COMING TO AMERICA

IRISH AMERICANS

COMING TO AMERICA

IRISH
AMERICANS

TOM DEIGNAN

Series editor: Barry Moreno

BARRON'S

First edition for the United States, its territories
and dependencies, and Canada published in 2003
by Barron's Educational Series, Inc.

Copyright © 2002 by
THE IVY PRESS LIMITED

This book was created by
The Ivy Press Ltd., The Old Candlemakers, Lewes, East Sussex BN7 2NZ, UK

Creative Director Peter Bridgewater
Publisher Sophie Collins
Editorial Director Steve Luck
Design Manager Tony Seddon
Designer Andrew Milne
Senior Project Editor Caroline Earle
Picture Researcher Vanessa Fletcher

All inquiries should be addressed to:
Barron's Educational Series, Inc.
250 Wireless Blvd.
Hauppauge, NY 11788

www.barronseduc.com

International Standard Book No.: 0-7641-5627-6

Library of Congress Catalog No.: 2002112399

Printed and bound in China by Hong Kong Graphics and Printing Ltd

9 8 7 6 5 4 3 2 1

CONTENTS

INTRODUCTION

ABOVE: *Throughout the United States and Ireland, memorials honor the Irish immigrant experience, to which 40 million Americans trace their ancestry.*

On January 1, 1892, a 15-year-old girl from County Cork named Annie Moore became the first immigrant to be processed at Ellis Island, the brand-new immigration facility in New York harbor. It is all too fitting that a "rosy cheeked Irish girl" (as the *The New York Times* described Annie) took these historic steps. The Irish, after all, had been crossing the Atlantic Ocean since the 1500s. It is simply impossible to imagine American history without the unique and vast contributions of Irish immigrants and their children. Presidents from Andrew Jackson to John F. Kennedy trace their roots to the Emerald Isle, as do hundreds of famous actors, writers, athletes, labor leaders, religious leaders, and tycoons. Overall, as many as 40 million Americans can claim Irish or Scotch-Irish ancestry.

However, the epic journey from rural Ireland to American prosperity was far from easy. Immigrants did not always leave Ireland by choice. Calamities such as the Irish Famine of 1845 to 1852 forced millions to huddle onto coffin ships and embark on a treacherous journey. Many of those lucky enough to survive the famine died on the high seas. Political turmoil and a depressed economy kept the Irish coming in the nineteenth and early twentieth centuries.

Those who did survive the trip were often met with hostility in America. Not only were the Irish

RIGHT: *JFK's grandfather Patrick J. Kennedy (seated, second from left) found success in Boston, after his father fled the terrible Irish Famine.*

poor foreigners, but the majority were Roman Catholics in a Protestant nation. In the 1830s and 1840s, Catholic churches in Irish ghettos were targeted by arsonists. The rampant anti-Irish discrimination is best captured by the oft-repeated slogan: "No Irish Need Apply."

As things turned out, however, the Irish did not necessarily need to apply. From San Francisco to New York, Irish immigrants banded together and rose up the social ladder. Some people sneered and accused the Irish of being clannish. However, the Irish understood the power of their numbers, seized upon the ballot box, and created the model for effective—and often corrupt—big-city political machines. Swiftly they also dominated police departments, granting Irish Americans the power

and respect that comes with the law. Their religious faith, meanwhile, provided a strong moral foundation as well as access to key social services, from medical care to education.

Just two decades after the famine ravaged Ireland, one in three New York City residents was of Irish descent. Cities such as Boston and Philadelphia also had large Irish-Catholic concentrations. Many were poor and despised. New York's infamous Draft Riots of 1863, three days of violence in which Irish immigrants played a dramatic role, symbolized Irish frustration and marginalization in big cities. Soon, however, immigrants and their children would be raising large families, producing girls who would go on to become teachers, and boys who would become police officers or maybe even lawyers. Other Irish came to prominence thanks to nineteenth-century

America's love of sport and entertainment. Boxers such as John Sullivan and "Gentleman" Jim Corbett dominated their field, while Tin Pan Alley churned out tunes deeply influenced by Irish music.

Perhaps it is a humble immigrant from County Wexford who best captures the spirit of the Irish immigrant experience. Patrick Kennedy left his farming family in the village of Dunganstown in 1849, eventually settling in Boston. Just over a century later, one of Patrick's many great-grandsons would become the first Roman Catholic president of the United States. The Kennedy clan, of course, faced tragedy and tribulations during that century. However, they were also widely seen as America's royal family, something Patrick Kennedy surely could not have imagined when he fled famine-ridden Ireland in 1849.

LEFT: *In the years after the famine, Irish immigrants and their children built up strong communities in American cities.*

RIGHT: *Boxing legend John L. Sullivan was one of many Irish Americans who excelled in the world of sport.*

RIGHT: *Parades on St. Patrick's Day remain enduring and popular symbols of the Irish in America.*

1600–1798
THE IRISH IN COLONIAL AMERICA

"GOD HAS OPENED A DOOR"

In 1737, immigrant James Murray wrote to friends in County Tyrone, "Tell [all] the poor folk of your place that God has opened a door for their deliverance."

Murray was writing from—and speaking of—America. Since the 1500s, this New World had been seen as a land of boundless opportunity for immigrants from Ireland. Irishmen (and, early on, it was mostly men) were part of the earliest expeditions to America. John Nugent joined Sir Walter Raleigh on his trip to North Carolina in the 1580s

LEFT: *Sir Walter Raleigh was accompanied by Irish immigrants during an expedition to America in the 1580s.*

and even "volunteered to kill Pemisapan, king of the Indians." Nugent carried out the dangerous mission, "and the Indians ceased their raids against the British camp," according to Captain John White's journal.

By the 1600s, however, many Irish were coming to America under dire circumstances. Some labored for years as indentured servants. Others were convicts or escapees of the religious wars that wracked Ireland during the seventeenth century. A large number of so-called Scotch-Irish also came to America from the ever-troubled northern region of Ireland, Ulster. They were rugged Presbyterians of Scottish descent and had been encouraged, as part of England's religious wars, to settle in northern Ireland. Many Irish Roman Catholics, meanwhile, were driven off their Ulster land.

Scotch-Irish fortunes in northern Ireland, however, were prey to the harsh seasons and fickle land. During the fierce winter of 1683 to 1684, as many as 2,000 Scotch-Irish fled Ulster for the Chesapeake Valley. Several Protestant ministers in County Donegal's Laggan Valley said that "general poverty abounding in these parts" forced them to emigrate in 1684.

ABOVE: *Tensions between Sir Walter Raleigh's crew and native Americans ran high. Irishman John Nugent eventually killed a warrior described as "king of the Indians" in battle.*

Scotch-Irish emigrated from Ulster during the seventeenth and eighteenth centuries.

Mass emigration occurred from 1785 to 1815, following the American Revolution.

From 1847 on, more than a million Irish emigrated during the famine years.

To save money, many Irish immigrants bound for America passed through Liverpool or other English ports, or through Canada.

É I R E

Atlantic Ocean

By the 1690s, one observer in Maryland found that Somerset County was "a place pestered with Scotch and Irish." The Scotch-Irish were so numerous because, often, entire families emigrated. Throughout the late sixteenth and early seventeenth centuries, landlords doubled—even tripled—rents on Ulster farms, "so that it is impossible to live or subsist," as one local archbishop observed.

So large Ulster families came to America, often setting out for the wilds of the American frontier.

Why? Generally cheap land was so abundant. In the minds of immigrants such as David Waugh, America was a place where former Ulster tenants could themselves become landlords. In a message published in the *Belfast Newsletter*, Waugh told "his countrymen that he can accommodate any of them that incline to go over with their families with farms of as good land as ever they enjoyed or saw in Ireland or perhaps better." Conditions in America, of course, were not always so generous.

Indentured servants labored particularly hard, especially Catholics from Ireland's southern region, who often faced discrimination at the hands of English settlers. Still, some Irish Catholics did thrive in America, such as the descendants of Charles Carroll, who settled in Maryland in the 1680s. His grandson Charles signed the Declaration of Independence and later served in the U.S. Senate, while his cousin John was America's first Catholic bishop.

By 1762, the Irish presence in America was already so strong that New York's first official St. Patrick's Day parade was held. As many as 10,000 Irish were emigrating annually before the announcement of the U.S. Declaration of Independence, a document that, fittingly, was printed by a successful immigrant from County Tyrone, John Dunlap. "The young men of Ireland who wish to be free and happy should leave it and come here as quick as possible," wrote Dunlap, who also started the United States' first daily newspaper, the *Pennsylvania Packet*. "There is no place in the world where a man meets so rich a reward for good conduct and industry as in America."

RIGHT: *George Washington was about to lead America into a revolutionary war for equality. However, many people in the American colonies discriminated against Irish-Catholic immigrants.*

IRISH PAPISTS ARRIVE

In 1654, the *Goodfellow* sailed into Boston harbor carrying hundreds of Irish men and women. They were swiftly sold into servitude. One local official,

Richard Mather, though, still feared the immigrants, decrying the influx of Irish as a "formidable attempt of Satan and his son to unsettle us." These Irish immigrants were Roman Catholics. Richard Mather's passionate opposition to their presence

ABOVE: *The Revolutionary War against the British began with the 1775 Battle of Lexington. The eventual American victory would later inspire soldiers in Ireland to rebel against British rule.*

illustrates the religious divisions that wracked America throughout the seventeenth and eighteenth centuries. In the long run, the Protestant–Catholic tension would profoundly affect the Irish immigrant experience.

America, of course, was a land founded on the basis of religious tolerance. However, since America (like Ireland) was a colony of Britain, it reflected many English attitudes and prejudices. Perhaps it was inevitable that Old World conflicts would be transported to the United States. After all, religious wars in Ireland—such as Oliver Cromwell's reign of terror during the 1640s—had been forcing Catholics (as well as Protestants) to flee for decades.

Just as some Irish Protestants thrived in America, so did prejudice against their Catholic countrymen. In 1704, Maryland levied a tax on indentured servants in an effort to lower the number of "Irish papists" in the region. Just before the war for American independence, Catholic worship was banned in all but Pennsylvania and parts of Maryland. By many accounts, this forced numerous Irish-Catholic immigrants to abandon their faith or to practice it in secret.

When the thirteen colonies' relationship with Britain deteriorated, religious differences were cast aside in significant ways. No less a revered figure than George Washington—many of whose Irish troops spoke only Gaelic—would later pray in honor of the Irish war effort in America.

GEORGE WASHINGTON

"Ireland, friend of my country in my country's most friendless days, much injured, much enduring land, accept this poor tribute from one who esteems thy worth, and mourns thy desolation."

LEFT: *Many Irish troops who served under George Washington during the Revolutionary War spoke only Gaelic.*

REVOLUTION
(IN IRELAND AND AMERICA)

Patrick Carr left Dublin and came to Boston to find a better life. Instead, on March 5, 1770, he became a martyr, one of five men gunned down during the infamous Boston Massacre.

From the start of the American Revolution, the Irish would clearly play a key role. Three of the 56 men who signed the American Declaration of Independence were Irish-born: Matthew Thornton,

George Taylor, and James Smith. (Irish-American Charles Carroll, however, was the only Catholic signatory of the Declaration.)

Wexford native John Barry became a captain in the U.S. Navy and went on to become "father of the U.S. Navy." Dublin native Richard Montgomery, a former officer in the British Army, moved to New York in 1772 and became a passionate advocate for American independence. He was killed in December 1775 during an assault in Quebec. America's small Irish-Catholic population, meanwhile, had a hero in Cork-born Stephen Moylan, a colonel on Washington's staff.

As is so often the case with the Irish in America, though, their involvement in the American Revolution was complicated. Many Irish were, in fact, loyal to Britain. Enlisting in the British Army was one way a poor Irishman could get to America, and groups such as the Volunteers of Ireland were fiercely loyal to the crown. The 1779 St. Patrick's Day parade in New York was even organized by an Irishman loyal to Britain.

The split loyalties of the Irish during the revolutionary years ultimately moved British commander in chief Sir Henry Clinton to say that the crown should draw strength from the same place that "the rebels themselves [draw] most of their support—I mean the Irish."

LEFT: *The terrible Boston Massacre on March 5, 1770 claimed an Irish victim, Patrick Carr from Dublin.*

LEFT: *Wolfe Tone was among the leaders of a 1798 rebellion in Ireland against British rule.*

BELOW: *Along with founding fathers such as Benjamin Franklin and Thomas Jefferson, prosperous Irish immigrants played a key role in formulating the Declaration of Independence.*

One thing is clear: the battle for American independence resonated with freedom fighters back in Ireland. In 1798, opponents of British rule in Ireland took a cue from America and also rebelled against their colonial leaders, with Wolfe Tone leading the way. The rebellion was unsuccessful. The ensuing Act of Union led to even harsher conditions of British rule in Ireland. However, 1798 would not be the last time Irish rebels were inspired by their brethren overseas in America.

1798 – 1845
EMBRACING THE NEW WORLD

ON THE FARM – AND IN THE WHITE HOUSE

Sixty-three years after his parents left County Antrim for the Irish settlement of Waxhaw in South Carolina, Andrew Jackson was elected president of the United States in 1828. Loathed by many elites, Jackson was a hero to many of America's common men and women. His admirers included thousands of Jackson's fellow Scotch-Irish, who were by and large farmers or artisans living far from America's rapidly growing, increasingly cosmopolitan cities.

Following the American Revolution, mass Irish immigration to America continued. Some 150,000 Irish poured into the United States from 1785 to 1815. They were still largely Presbyterians from northern Ireland. By the dawn of the nineteenth century, however, these sturdy men and women were moving not only to Virginia or the Carolinas. The West also beckoned many Irish families, such as the O'Hares. An Ulster native, Catherine O'Hare, bore a child believed to be the first of Irish descent west of the Rockies in 1802.

County Donegal immigrant James Crockett and his wife Hannah purchased more than 100 acres of land in western Pennsylvania after Crockett struggled for nearly 20 years as a Philadelphia stonemason. In an 1822 letter to his father back in Ireland, Crockett described the grueling labor required to maintain a farm in America. He also spoke, though, with joy of American freedom and with bitterness about dastardly landlords in Ireland:

"Twelve years ago, for $2.00 an acre, I bought the land where I now live. It looked a wild, uncultivated place to make a living, nothing but trees and bushes to be seen. But I went to work with my axe and grubbing hoe, and soon felled as many trees as would build a house and clear enough ground for our first crop. It is killing on nature to work outdoors in this country, the summers are so hot and the winters so cold, but I now have 30 acres cleared, 20 cattle, and a good harvest. We are happy and contented. Our house is small but our barn is full. Thank God I came to this country where we are free from landlords, rent, and the fear of eviction."

LEFT: *Many Scotch-Irish immigrants were lured to America with promises of cheap, plentiful land in the southern and western frontier territories.*

ABOVE: *The open spaces of the American frontier were attractive to Irish immigrants, who were often driven from their farms in Ireland by high prices, political upheaval, or greedy landlords.*

BELOW: *Many Irish were in
attendance when Andrew
Jackson was inaugurated.
The Irish embraced Jackson,
who extolled the virtues of
hard work, particularly on
the frontier, where many
Scotch-Irish farmers had settled.*

RIGHT: *The son of Scotch-Irish
immigrants, Andrew Jackson
served in the U.S. Army before
becoming the seventh president of
the United States. He was
widely regarded as a champion
of the common man, who helped
to shape the Democratic Party.*

ANDREW JACKSON.
Seventh President of the United States.

Crockett was just the kind of man likely to vote for that proud son of Ulster, Andrew Jackson, when he captured the White House in 1828. Jackson—a war hero who, at 13, brawled with a British soldier during the Revolutionary War—appealed to the decency of the hard-working common person. At a pro-Jackson rally in Boston, one observer noted, "Proclaiming Jackson as an Irishman, [Jackson supporters held] him up as the champion of the poor against the rich, they received with 'hugs fraternal' the tenants of poorhouses and penitentiaries." To Irish immigrants, both on the farms and in the cities,

Jackson's humble roots and passion for the underdog made the seventh president a folk hero. Jackson also cemented what would become a long Irish association with the Democratic Party.

Life in the United States remained trying for many Irish immigrants. More often than not, at the very least, things were better in America than they were in the old country. Jackson himself expressed this sentiment in one speech, proclaiming, "Would to God, sir, that Irishmen on the other side of the great water enjoyed the comforts, happiness, contentment, and liberty that we enjoy here."

RIGHT: *There was plenty of land in America for Irish immigrants, but there were many dangers as well. Families such as this had to watch out for perils ranging from hostile Native Americans to harsh winters.*

"MICKS WITH PICKS"

> *"Ten Thousand Micks, they swung*
> *their picks,*
> *To dig the new canal.*
> *But the choleray was stronger 'n they,*
> *An' twice it killed them all."*

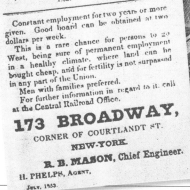

BELOW: *Many Irish were also lured to the United States with offers of plentiful work and high pay. Railroad projects were particularly attractive to Irish immigrant laborers.*

This mournful ballad was sung by Irish workers outside New Orleans. However, the tune would also have resonated with thousands of immigrants in early nineteenth-century America for whom farming was not an option. Despite the era's burgeoning stereotype of the lazy Irish, immigrant laborers worked from sunup to sundown in treacherous conditions. One Irish visitor to an 1830s Louisiana camp site reported, "[Irish workers were] wheeling, digging, hewing, or bearing burdens it made one's shoulders ache to look upon."

By 1818, as many as 3,000 Irish were digging the Erie Canal in upstate New York; by 1834, the Chesapeake and Ohio Canal (C&O) employed nearly 2,000 Irish laborers. Other canal projects sent immigrants west and even south. "To dig a canal, at least four things are necessary," a saying of the time went, "a shovel, a pick, a wheelbarrow, and an Irishman."

WANTED!
3,000 LABORERS
On the 12th Division of the
ILLINOIS CENTRAL RAILROAD
Wages, $1.25 per Day.
Fare, from New-York, only - - $4.75
By Railroad and Steamboat, to the work in the
State of Illinois.

Constant employment for two years or more given. Good board can be obtained at two dollars per week.

This is a rare chance for persons to go West, being sure of permanent employment in a healthy climate, where land can be bought cheap, and for fertility is not surpassed in any part of the Union.

Men with families preferred.

For further information in regard to it, call at the Central Railroad Office.

173 BROADWAY,
CORNER OF COURTLANDT ST.
NEW-YORK.
R. B. MASON, Chief Engineer.
H. PHELPS, Agent.
July, 1853.

ABOVE: *The expansion of the railroad system in the United States not only meant more jobs for Irish laborers; it also enabled immigrants to find jobs— and homes—all across the country.*

LEFT: *Irish laborers on railroad projects worked under extremely harsh conditions. Often, laborers suffered fatal injuries or contracted terrible diseases.*

Gruesomely, some projects were considered so dangerous by southern slave owners that they did not want to risk losing their "property," and so they hired "disposable" Irish immigrants instead.

So crucial was Irish labor that U.S. companies sent word of plentiful work and high wages across the Atlantic to Ireland. By the early nineteenth century, farmers in Ireland had seen their rents raised astronomically by landlords. Their peasant way of life, maintained by subsistence farming, had all but vanished. When business titans such as the president of the C&O came calling, the Irish were willing to listen. "Meat three times a day, a plenty of bread and vegetables, with a reasonable allowance of liquor and light, ten, or twelve dollars a month wages" were promised by the C&O executive.

What he did not talk about, of course, were the rampant malaria, typhoid, cholera, and other deadly diseases. In 1843, Edward Hanlon, from County Down, went to the "Grand River, where over 2,000 men, most of them Irish, were digging a great canal," he wrote. "In 4 weeks over 150 of my workmates died, shaking with fever, with about 700 more lying sick. Never did I feel so much the loss of my dear parents—or the want of a Catholic clergyman, for there were none within 50 miles." The homes of Irish laborers were often shanties

near the work site, which, at desperate times, would even be shared with horses or pigs.

Later in the nineteenth century, when many Irish gravitated to coal mining, there were the lethal effects of explosions to contend with, not to mention the disdain of native-born locals, who would hang out signs reading, "No Dogs or Irish Permitted." Still, the bosses were right about one thing: work was plentiful. With American-born workers uninterested in the backbreaking canal or mine work, pay was relatively high—as much as $20 a month on some western canals. By the time the Erie Canal was completed in 1826, 5,000 Irish laborers had worked on what would be the young nation's most important transportation project.

A distinctly Irish sense of community pervaded what were sometimes called Corktowns (if the Irish workers came from Cork or other southern Irish regions). Some workers married and settled in towns such as Akron, Ohio, where Irish traditions took root, even when the work dried up. Generally, however, laborers were forced to become *spalpeens* (as the old Gaelic called itinerant laborers).

The fiercely masculine culture of the work camps could lead to excessive drinking and brawling. However, the hard labor also prodded many Irish to band together for higher wages or better conditions in these boom years of canal building and mining. It was the start of a proud organized labor tradition among Irish Americans, who could say that they were literally building a new nation.

FAR LEFT: *Many Irish settled in industrial towns bringing with them many customs, including a devotion to the Catholic Church.*

LEFT: *Workers on a Pennsylvania coal site, 1911. Coal mining was a popular—and dangerous—job among Irish immigrants.*

IN THE CITY

Robert Brunt was raised a farmer in Ireland. He came to New York in 1817. By 1833, he was a successful big-city entrepreneur. He employed many fellow Irish immigrants to do the grimy but necessary work of removing dirt for construction projects in northern Manhattan. Brunt and his team of Irish laborers are part of an oft-forgotten wave of Irish immigration. As many as 1 million Irish came to the United States in the decades prior to the Great Famine.

By the 1830s, more and more immigrants from Ireland were poor Catholics from southern and western Ireland, many of whom still spoke Gaelic. Small rural farmers had been hard hit not only by rising rents but by famines in 1817, 1822, and 1831. At the same time, Ireland was undergoing an astonishing growth in population, from 6.8 million

ABOVE: *Daniel O'Connell became a folk hero in Ireland because of his fight for Catholic equal rights. In 1829, O'Connell's efforts compelled British authorities to pass the Catholic Emancipation Act.*

in 1821 to more than 8 million by 1840. The obvious choice for many seeking work at this time was to go to "Americkay."

Interestingly, Catholic immigration to America swelled just as Catholics were gaining equal rights in Ireland. Following the restrictive Act of Union in 1800, Catholics in Ireland began a long struggle for civil rights. Led by the charismatic Daniel O'Connell, they fought laws denying them basic rights such as voting and land ownership. On April 13, 1829, the Catholic Emancipation Act became law, essentially making Catholics equal to Protestants. However, a movement to repeal the Act of Ireland, so that Ireland could govern itself, fell apart.

Despite the political gains in Ireland, immigration remained the only hope for many rural Catholics. From 1820 to 1920, three out of four Irish immigrants to the United States were Catholic. Lacking the money and more diverse agricultural skills of other immigrants attracted to the open land on the frontier, Irish-Catholic immigrants settled for hard labor in urban America. For men, that meant building and manning the factories in Boston or Lowell, Massachusetts. For women, it meant long days as seamstresses or domestic servants for contemptuous, upper-class Protestant families.

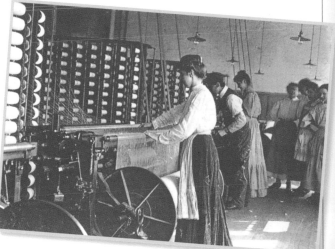

ABOVE RIGHT: *Irish women performed harsh jobs, such as shelling nuts. Since they used their teeth, the spread of tuberculosis was rampant.*

RIGHT: *Many Irish immigrant women found work in textile factories, such as this mill in Newberry, South Carolina.*

ABOVE: *Anti-Catholic riots were a fact of life in Irish immigrant neighborhoods beginning in the 1830s. This was still the case in 1871, when Irish Protestants and Catholics in New York clashed in what came to be called "The Orange Riots."*

With so many Irish Catholics settling in the cities, entire neighborhoods were transformed. Immigrants flocked to local saloons (often recently opened by fellow Irishmen) for camaraderie, for politics, or to forget their troubles. Clergymen such as Father Philip Lariscy were beloved in Brooklyn and Philadelphia because they heard confessions in Gaelic, just as Father Jeremiah O'Callaghan did in Lowell. Meanwhile, Irish workers called the first organized strike in a large U.S. city. In 1835, 300 Philadelphia coal heavers went on strike and called for a ten-hour day. Poor Irish ghettos eventually formed in many northeastern cities, and anti-Irish and anti-Catholic prejudices resurfaced. In 1834, a mob torched the Ursuline convent in Charlestown, Massachusetts. And in Philadelphia, a decade later, Irish homes, two Catholic churches, and a seminary belonging to the Sisters of Mercy were all burned to the ground.

This came on top of the trials and tribulations of adjusting to life in the big city. To assist immigrants, Irish benevolent groups—such as the Hibernian Society of Baltimore and the Shamrock Friendly Association of New York—sprang up. The first known Irish-American newspaper, New York's *The Shamrock*, was founded in 1810 by an exile of the 1798 rebellion. Given the religious troubles of the era, it comes as no surprise that in 1836 the first Ancient Order of Hibernians charter in the United States was granted. This secret sixteenth-century organization was founded in Ireland to protect Catholics (among other things).

The journey overseas to the United States was certainly harsh. Still, ships were constantly carting immigrants from Ireland to America, or throughout Europe. On one of these ships was a disease known technically as *Phytophthera infestans*. This contagion, known to be particularly harmful to potato crops, was eventually carried to Ireland, where it would soon alter the course of world history.

LEFT: *The number of ships carrying Irish immigrants across the Atlantic increased steadily during the first half of the nineteenth century. Tragically, one of them made the return journey carrying the disease that would decimate Ireland's potato crops.*

1845–1865
THE FAMINE YEARS

AN GORTA MÓR
(THE GREAT HUNGER)

William Bennet was a Quaker who spent time in the west of Ireland in 1847 at the height of the terrible Irish Famine, or *an Gorta Mór* (uh GOR-ta more), as it is referred to in Gaelic, meaning "The Great Hunger."

"We entered a cabin," Bennet later wrote describing the scene. "Stretched in one dark corner, scarcely visible, from the smoke and rags that covered them, were three children huddled together, lying there because they were too weak to rise, pale and ghastly their little limbs—on removing a portion of the filthy covering—perfectly emaciated eyes sunk, voice gone and in the last stage of starvation."

The horrors of the Irish Famine, which lasted from 1845 to 1852, killed more than 1 million Irish men, women, and children, and sent another million across the globe. Just before the reports of a potato blight became public, in the early 1840s, Ireland's population was 8 million; by 1861 it had fallen to 5.8 million. For decades after the famine, Ireland's population would dwindle, shrunk by both death and immigration.

BELOW: *Irish farmers, too poor to pay their rent during the famine, were often evicted from their modest homes by indifferent landlords. Emigration over the Atlantic Ocean became the only option for many.*

ABOVE: *Artist George Frederick Watts attempted to capture the suffering of the Irish Famine, which killed a million Irish people and sent a million immigrants across the globe.*

FAR LEFT: *Many Irish were driven to living in hovels during the terrible famine of the 1840s.*

While premature death and immigration shrunk Ireland's population, the number of Irish in America grew at a remarkable rate. By 1850, nearly a million Irish-born people lived in the United States. By 1860, that number had grown to 1.6 million. As prefamine Catholic immigrants had done, the famine's escapees flocked to northeastern cities such as Philadelphia, Boston, and New York. An estimated 848,000 Irish immigrants came to New York from 1847 to 1851; more than 53,000 arrived from May to December 1847, or "black '47," as the worst year of the famine was often called.

The great starvation that decimated Ireland was the result of an astonishing combination of forces:

PASSENGERS' CONTRACT TICKET.

No. 27.

465

55-504

Ship *Princeton* of 1000 tons register burthen, to sail from Liverpool, for *New York* on the *Twenty Eighth* Day of *May* 1851

I engage that the Parties herein named shall be provided with a Steerage Passage to the Port of *New York* in the United States of America, in the Ship *Princeton* with not less than Ten Cubic Feet for Luggage for each Statute Adult, for the Sum of £ 3 – 5 – 0 including Government Dues before Embarkation, and Head Money, if any, at the place of landing, and every other charge ; and I hereby acknowledge to have received the sum of £ 3 . 5 . 0 in full payment.

NAMES.	AGES.	NO. OF STATUTE ADULTS.

British neglect, Irish reliance on the potato, and a contagion introduced to Ireland by a ship that had passed through America. During the wet summer of 1845, Irish potato fields appeared to be thriving. One Dublin newspaper, the *Freeman's Journal*, reported the story of a farmer who "had been digging potatoes—the finest he had ever seen—up to Monday last." The next day, however, his potatoes were "unfit for the use of man or beast."

As many as 3 million of Ireland's 8 million people lived almost solely on the potato, literally eating pounds daily. It was the only food that many of the poorest farmers in the west and south of Ireland could afford. As tenants beholden to landlords, their remaining crops were used to pay the rent. Once the fungus *Phytophthera infestans* struck their prized crop, a chain of events was set in motion that would result in one of the worst tragedies in world history.

ABOVE: *The famine was, in some ways, a boon to shipping companies, who could exploit desperate Irish immigrants. Rarely did advertisements mention the dangerous nature of the trip across the Atlantic.*

BELOW: *Conditions on some ships during the famine were so wretched that they came to be known as "coffin ships."*

Entire villages, particularly in the rural, Gaelic-speaking south and west of Ireland, were abandoned. "I was told that Sligo emigrants left home in secret," one descendant of famine survivors recalled. "They went onboard the ship at the dead of night. They said if the emigrants went in the daytime and if the landlord knew of their going, he might hold them and take from them money and everything else they had."

As the famine worsened, landlords were granted the power simply to evict tenants, leaving them without shelter or food. It was not uncommon to see starving or dead adults and children lining rural Irish roads during the famine. Widowed Bridget Nolan and her five children were among those evicted. She wrote to her son, who had earlier emigrated to Rhode Island:

"This is the poorest winter that ever I had since I began the world, without house nor home nor a bit of food to eat. The potato crops have failed again, and all Ireland is dying. Your sisters are fainting with starvation, and we are without friend or fellow to give us a shilling. For God's sake, have pity on us! On my two bended knees I pray—take us out of this gulf of misery and save us from the hunger."

The response of British leaders to the suffering in its colony has been heavily criticized, with many saying that the British caused, or encouraged, the "Irish holocaust." British assistant secretary to the treasury, Charles Trevelyan, who was put in charge of famine relief in July 1846, argued that God must have sent the potato blight to encourage the "moral and political improvement" of the Irish. Others said the Irish deserved the famine for their devout Catholicism, adding that simply to give food to the starving Irish would only make them lazy.

As negligent as the British were, there were modest efforts by the British government to feed the Irish. In the end, though, 300 years of British rule had left many Irish Catholics vulnerable and beholden to wealthy Protestant landowners. It seemed as if all they had was the potato, producing 15 million tons a year just before the famine; afterward, just 2 million tons were harvested.

It did not help that the famine years saw upheaval within the British government itself. So, while the politicians bickered and debated, the "scattered debris of the Irish nation" (as New York archbishop John Hughes put it) was going to America. Future generations on both sides of the Atlantic would be haunted by the famine, which would forever taint immigrant views of the old country.

In the bitter folk tune "Skibbereen," named after the district in Cork most hard hit by the famine, a father sings:

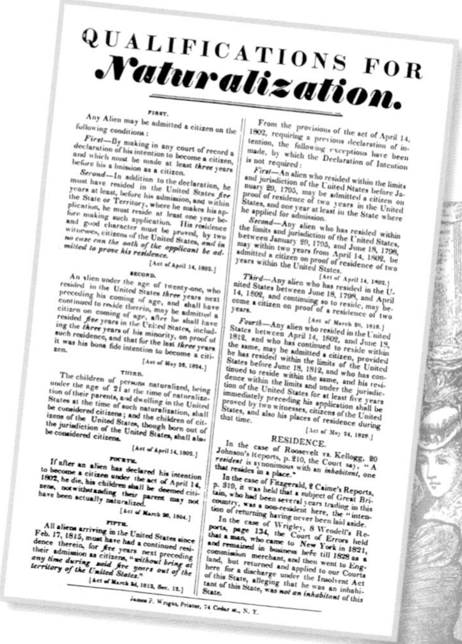

QUALIFICATIONS FOR *Naturalization.*

FIRST.

Any Alien may be admitted a citizen on the following conditions:

First—By making in any court of record a declaration of his intention to become a citizen, and which must be made at least *three* years before his admission as a citizen.

Second—In addition to the declaration, he must have resided in the United States *five* years at least, before his admission, and within the State or Territory, where he makes his application, he must reside at least one year before making such application. His residence and good character must be proved, by two witnesses, citizens of the United States, *and in no case can the oath of the applicant be admitted to prove his residence.*

[Act of April 14, 1802.]

SECOND.

An alien under the age of twenty-one, who resided in the United States *three* years next preceding his coming of age, and shall have continued to reside therein, may be admitted a citizen on coming of age, after he shall have resided *five* years in the United States, including the *three* years of his minority, on proof of such residence, and that for the last *three* years it was his bona fide intention to become a citizen.

[Act of May 26, 1824.]

THIRD.

The children of persons naturalized, being under the age of 21 at the time of naturalization of their parents, and dwelling in the United States at the time of such naturalization, shall be considered citizens; and the children of citizens of the United States, though born out of the jurisdiction of the United States, shall also be considered citizens.

[Act of April 14, 1802.]

FOURTH.

If after an alien has declared his intention to become a citizen under the act of April 14, 1802, he die, his children shall be deemed citizens, notwithstanding their parent may not have been actually naturalized.

[Act of March 26, 1804.]

FIFTH.

All aliens arriving in the United States since Feb. 17, 1815, must have had a continued residence therein, for *five* years next preceding their admission as citizens, "*without being at any time during said five years out of the territory of the United States.*"

[Act of March 3d, 1813, Sec. 12.]

From the provisions of the act of April 14, 1802, requiring a previous declaration of intention, the following exceptions have been made, by which the Declaration of Intention is not required:

First—An alien who resided within the limits and jurisdiction of the United States before January 29, 1795, may be admitted a citizen on proof of residence of two years in the United States, and one year at least in the State where he applied for admission.

Second—Any alien who has resided within the limits and jurisdiction of the United States, between January 29, 1795, and June 18, 1798, may within two years from April 14, 1802, be admitted a citizen on proof of residence of two years within the United States.

[Act of April 14, 1802.]

Third—Any alien who has resided in the United States between June 18, 1798, and April 14, 1802, and continuing so to reside, may become a citizen on proof of a residence of two years.

[Act of March 26, 1816.]

Fourth—Any alien who resided in the United States between April 14, 1802, and June 18, 1812, and who has continued to reside within the same, may be admitted a citizen, provided he has resided within the limits of the United States before June 18, 1812, and who has continued to reside within the same, and his residence within the limits and under the jurisdiction of the United States for at least five years immediately preceding his application shall be proved by two witnesses, citizens of the United States, and also his places of residence during that time.

[Act of May 24, 1828.]

RESIDENCE.

In the case of Roosevelt vs. Kellogg, 20 Johnson's Reports, p. 210, the Court say, "A *resident* is synonimous with an *inhabitant*, one that resides in a place."

In the case of Fitzgerald, 2 Caime's Reports, p. 319, it was held that a subject of Great Britain, who had been several years trading in this country, was a non-resident here, the "intention of returning having never been laid aside.

In the case of Wrigley, 8 Wendell's Reports, page 134, the Court of Errors held that a man, who came to New York in 1821, and remained in business here till 1828 as a commission merchant, and then went to England, but returned and applied to our Courts here for a discharge under the Insolvent Act of this State, alleging that he was an inhabitant of this State, was *not an inhabitant* of this State.

James P. Wright, Printer, 74 Cedar st., N. Y.

LEFT: *Irish immigrants looking to become citizens had to meet many requirements—although political organizations were often helpful in cutting red tape (as long, of course, as the Irish voted for certain political candidates).*

BELOW: *A group of impoverished Irish immigrants wait dockside to board a ship bound for New York. For those who survived the treacherous journey, there were new hardships to face once they arrived in America.*

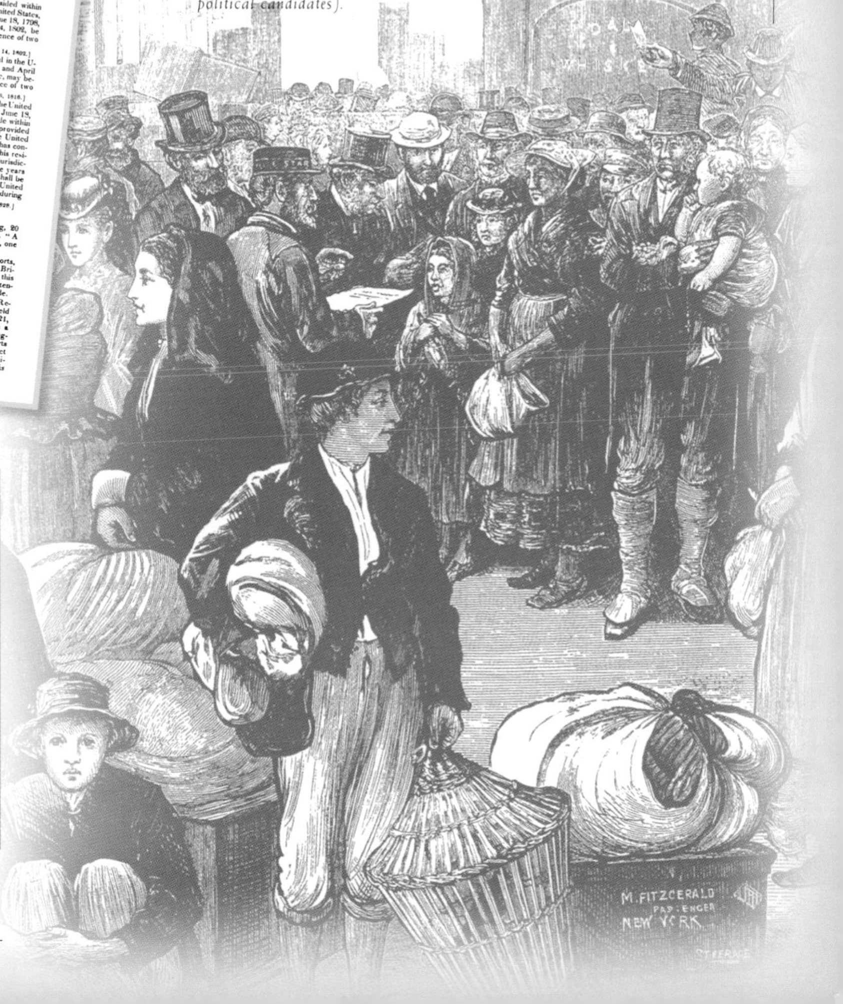

"Oh son! I loved my native land
with energy and pride.
Till a blight came o'er my crops—
my sheep, my cattle died.
My rent and taxes were too high,
I could not them redeem,
And that's the cruel reason why
I left old Skibbereen."

ABOVE: *It was not uncommon for Irish immigrants to spend weeks on a cramped "coffin ship," with little food and a high rate of disease.*

COFFIN SHIPS

"It was a charming morning on which I left dear old Ireland," Robert Whyte wrote in his diary, as he boarded a ship in 1847. "It was a morning calculated to inspire the drooping soul with hope auguring future happiness."

The Atlantic Ocean was the only hope for hundreds of thousands of Irish escaping the Great Famine. However, the death and disease of abandoned Irish cottages seemed to follow the Irish onto their ships. So crowded and infested were these vessels that they became known as coffin ships. Immigrants spent weeks at a time on the treacherous seas, hundreds of them crammed into foul-smelling quarters, with uncaring crews on board.

To save money, many Irish bound for America passed through Liverpool or other English ports, or through Canada, but these more affordable boats could also be more dangerous. Most notoriously, at the Canadian port of Grosse Isle, 5,500 Irish immigrants officially arrived dead during the famine. It is believed, however, that as many as 15,000 actually died at Grosse Isle, where nearly 50 Canadian medical personnel also died after contracting diseases.

Some coffin ships filled with 400 people ultimately reached America with only 150 living Irish souls. So many Irish eventually contracted tuberculosis that it became known as "the natural death of the Irish." In 1849, Henry David Thoreau

stumbled upon recent Irish immigrants picking their way through the wreckage of what was once the ship *St. John*. It had left Galway in Ireland but sailed into a vicious storm and broke apart just a mile from Boston harbor. "All their plans and hopes burst like a bubble," the great American author wrote in horror. "Infants by the score dashed on the rocks by the enraged Atlantic Ocean. No! No!"

BELOW: *The conditions at Canada's Grosse Isle immigrant port were infamous. As many as 15,000 Irish may have died upon landing after contracting diseases at the port.*

The
Grosse-Isle Tragedy
and the
Monument to the Irish Fever Victims
1847

REPRINTED, WITH ADDITIONAL INFORMATION AND ILLUSTRATIONS, FROM THE DAILY TELEGRAPH'S COMMEMORATIVE SOUVENIR, ISSUED ON THE OCCASION OF THE UNVEILING OF THE NATIONAL MEMORIAL ON THE 15TH AUGUST 1909, INCLUDING A FULL ACCOUNT OF THE DEDICATORY CEREMONIES, SERMON, SPEECHES, ETC.

By J. A. Jordan

HOUSE LIBRARY
LOYOLA COLLEGE, MONTREAL

Quebec
Published and Printed by
The Telegraph Printing Company
H. D. Nineteen Hundred and Nine

> "Do not fret that I have forgotten you and our little ones," Martin O'Gara wrote home to his wife and four children in 1848. "I have saved £5 [about $25] which I now send you to feed the children. With the help of God in my next letter I will pay your passage and bring you all to join me in this land of plenty."

ENTERING AMERICA

With passage tickets costing as much as $50, many Irish families had to come to the United States one at a time. It is estimated that some $300 million was sent from America back to Ireland in the mid-nineteenth century, when the Emigrant Industrial Savings Bank was founded by the Irish Emigrant Society to administer this commercial exchange, as well as encourage savings.

The most popular destination for Irish immigrants during this era was New York's Castle Garden, where nearly 2 million Irish arrived in the 30 years after the famine. Unlike the more strict procedures at Ellis Island (which was not opened until 1892), at Castle Garden Irish immigrants were generally given merely a quick inspection. As a result, some immigrant illnesses were not diagnosed until much later.

For those who managed to survive the treacherous journey, new hazards awaited on the streets of Boston, Chicago, or Manhattan. Right off the boat, immigrants were approached by men aiming to lure newcomers to certain businesses—or to size them up as targets for burglary. Known as runners, these men might affect a perfect Irish accent or even speak Gaelic. However, one safeguard that many Irish immigrants had against criminally inclined runners was that immigrants rarely brought with them much more than the ragged clothes on their backs.

Aside from the cramped ship conditions, which put a premium on space, precious items were often sold in Ireland in order to finance emigration. The Irish did, of course, carry with them a vibrant tradition of story and song, of hard work and ancient tradition. Consider Halloween, for instance, the holiday that evolved from the ancient Celtic celebration of Samhain. No mere runner could snatch such traditions away.

ABOVE: *This 1855 painting captures the scene of an Irish immigrant ship docking at an American port.*

RIGHT: *Most Irish immigrants during the famine entered America through Castle Garden, in downtown Manhattan.*

RIGHT: *Upon landing, immigrants were often greeted by "runners," who offered their assistance. A runner's motives, however, were rarely pure.*

THE AMERICAN CLACHAN

Irish immigrants to the United States were unique in a number of ways. These thoroughly rural people were forced to adjust from life in the traditional close-knit Irish village (*clachan* in Gaelic) to life on the teeming streets and in the packed tenements of America. It was natural, therefore, for many Irish-Catholic immigrants to stick together,

RIGHT: *"Dagger" John Hughes was a parish priest to thousands of New York's famine immigrants. He was not afraid to rattle the Protestant establishment.*

recreating in a way the clachan in the close quarters of city neighborhoods in the United States. The famine immigrants were the first large-scale wave of foreigners to wash up on American shores in such concentrated numbers (as opposed to slaves, who were of course dragged to the United States) and whereas immigrants from other countries were typically male, female immigrants from Ireland actually made up more than half the Irish during the peak post-famine immigration years.

In places such as Chicago, the Irish were swiftly dismissed as lazy and shiftless—despite evidence to the contrary. "Who does not know that the most depraved, debased, worthless, and irredeemable drunkards and sots which curse the community are Irish Catholics?" the *Chicago Tribune* sneered. This even as Irish laborers worked feverishly to complete Chicago's stately St. Patrick's Church in 1855.

One man determined to change such bigoted attitudes was New York archbishop "Dagger" John Hughes, whose nickname came from the prominent knifelike crucifix that he wore (and he often included a cross when he signed his name). A sort of parish priest to thousands of New York Irish, Hughes was not afraid to rattle the Protestant establishment, whether the issue was protection from anti-Irish mobs or funds for the fledgling Catholic schools system. At the same time, Hughes (born in Tyrone) demanded that his impoverished flock live a pious life in the New World. He then set out to expand the number of Catholic schools,

LEFT AND ABOVE: *New York's famous St. Patrick's Cathedral was built in the wake of the Irish Famine. (The twin spires were added in* *the 1880s.) It was just one of Archbishop Hughes' many ambitious construction projects.*

hospitals, and churches in New York. His grand achievement was the construction of the landmark St. Patrick's Cathedral on Manhattan's Fifth Avenue. The foundations laid by Hughes and his followers would support the Irish in those great clachans of Boston, Chicago, Philadelphia, and New York for more than a century.

BELOW: *New York's Five Points district was a bustling, notoriously dangerous Irish neighborhood when it was rendered by an unknown artist during the 1840s. But many Irish in the neighborhood were, in fact, hard-working and devout immigrants who built stable lives for themselves.*

"I'm a decent boy just landed
from the town of Ballyfad
I want a situation and I
want it very bad.
I have seen employment
advertised, 'It's just the
thing,' says I
But the dirty ad ended with
'No Irish Need Apply!'"

"No Irish Need Apply"

The prevalence of such anti-Irish notices has been the subject of some exaggeration. However, anti-Irish sentiment was clearly strong in the United States in the years following the Great Famine. Not only were the famine-struck Irish overwhelmingly Catholic, but they were also the poorest of the poor, packed into dangerous urban ghettos. In New York's Five Points district, "Poverty, wretchedness, and vice are rife," as Charles Dickens wrote when he visited in the 1840s.

Some Five Points Irish did forge stable new lives. At Transfiguration Roman Catholic Church, more than 1,000 Irish immigrants—half of them from the western Irish counties of Sligo, Cork, and Kerry—married from 1853 to 1860. Many immigrants also shook the hands of Democratic Party ward heelers, who promised food and shelter in exchange for votes.

Still, Irish ghettos were often wretched places. A Boston health commission found immigrants "huddled together like brutes, without regard to sex or age, or sense of decency." Disease and violence flourished amid this poverty. As a result, Irish immigrants were stereotyped as lazy, drunken criminals. Acclaimed *Harper's* illustrator Thomas Nast

regularly depicted the Irish as apelike creatures slavishly dedicated to the Democratic Party and the pope in Rome. Perhaps the era's most notorious symbol of anti-Irish sentiment was the so-called Know Nothing political party, which flourished nationwide in the 1850s on an anti-immigrant, anti-Catholic platform.

Amid this turmoil it was easy to forget Wexford immigrants such as Bridget and Pat Kennedy, who had met on the ship *Washington Irving*, married, and settled in Boston. Pat became a hard-working cooper, a father of four, and the founder of what would become the great American political dynasty.

RIGHT: *Thomas Nast was one of many newspaper illustrators whose hatred for the Irish was evident in his many cartoons for* Harper's. *The Irish (as this cartoon suggests) were thought to be apelike, violent drunkards.*

THE USUAL IRISH WAY OF DOING THINGS.

"The Venerable Tongue of Our Beloved Fatherland"

In 1848, as famine-stricken Irish poured into America, New York State passed a law requiring boarding houses to post their rates in the "English, German, Dutch, French, and Welsh language." No mention of Gaelic was made, suggesting that the language had already all but vanished, or that the Irish were being ignored.

While British colonialism, illiteracy, assimilation, and other factors had made Gaelic less important, many Irish did come to America as Gaelic speakers. As far back as 1688, washerwoman and accused witch Goody Glover gave testimony at her trial in Gaelic (she was eventually hanged). The runners who sought to lure immigrants at ports often implemented their schemes because they spoke fluent Gaelic. Some estimates suggest that as many as 30 percent of mid-nineteenth-century immigrants spoke Gaelic. In 1857, the New York-based *Irish American* newspaper even introduced a new Gaelic column, a feature that no paper in Ireland offered.

LEFT: *Boarding houses catering to all kinds of immigrants were not required to post their rates in the Irish-Gaelic language, but the language was still spoken by Irish boarders.*

RIGHT: *Some very shrewd "runners" who greeted Irish immigrants did so speaking in Gaelic. The Irish language was still spoken quite widely in the mid-nineteenth century.*

Of course, Gaelic was a waning language, even in the 1800s. However, it was a language that never died. Even if it was merely out of spite—given that the English had "stolen" their language—many Irish continued to cling to what one observer called "the venerable tongue of our beloved fatherland." Into the 1970s, 45,000 Irish immigrants in the United States claimed to speak Gaelic in their homes; by the 1980s, 20,000 still called it their mother tongue. Plays or masses in Gaelic still draw crowds in Irish enclaves, and the 1990s saw a huge growth in the number of Gaelic cultural groups and college courses.

RIGHT: *For rural Irish immigrants who spoke only Gaelic, Robert McDougall produced this "Emigrant's Guide to North America" in 1841.*

CEANN-IÙIL AN FHIR-IMRICH DO DH'AMERICA MU-THUATH;

OR,

THE EMIGRANT'S GUIDE TO NORTH AMERICA.

By ROBERT M'DOUGALL, Esq.

Ni fear a dh'fhalbhas 'na thràth
Biadh 'us bòrr 'nam bi toirt ;
Am feadh bhios tàchrnig gun stàth,
A' dul bàs leis a ghort :
Bithidh piseach agus lainn
Air a chloinn 'n air a mhunaidh ;
Am feadh bhios truaghanin gun guinn,
Fo na Goill air an cluaidh.

GLASGOW:
J. & P. CAMPBELL, 34, GLASSFORD STREET,
OBAN : J. MILLER.—INVERNESS : J. BAIN & CO.
DINGWALL : A. KEITH.

MDCCCXLI.

ABOVE: *Immigrants played a key role in the U.S. Civil War, with nearly 150,000 Irish-born soldiers fighting for the Union army alone. Michael Corcoran's aim was to recruit Irish civil war veterans to fight in later battles for freedom in Ireland.*

RIGHT: *Thomas Francis Meagher was a Civil War hero and famous member of the "The Fighting 69th," an all-Irish brigade formed in 1851.*

THE FIGHTING 69TH

Bigots who said the Irish could never be true Americans had never met the likes of Bridget Diver. Irish Bridget, as she was known, served alongside her husband as a nurse in the 1st Michigan Cavalry during the U.S. Civil War. "Bate the bloody spaleens and avenge my husband," she is said to have roared to retreating Union soldiers as she tended her wounded husband during the Battle of Fair Oaks—not the first time Bridget rallied the troops under fire.

During the bloody war from 1861 to 1865, which left some 600,000 dead, Irish soldiers were some of the most courageous fighters. Nearly 150,000 Irish-born soldiers fought for the Union Army alone (with another 30,000, it is estimated, fighting for the South). Perhaps the most famous Irish regiment was the Fighting 69th, an all-Irish unit formed in 1851 of Irish revolutionary exiles, such as its Brigadier General Thomas Francis Meagher. Ulster native Michael Corcoran, who rose to the rank of colonel, hoped to train Fighting 69th immigrants to fight later for freedom in Ireland.

Less well-known Irish Civil War heroes include Belfast-born Jenny Hodgers. Incredibly, Hodgers enlisted in Company G of the 95th Illinois Volunteer Infantry disguised as a man. Her true gender was not discovered until she was committed to an insane asylum at the age of 70. When Jenny died, she was given full military honors.

Perhaps the most important aspect of the Civil War for the Irish was giving them a chance to fight for America. As a result, not only did these "foreigners" come to feel more American, but native-born Americans came to realize that immigrants could make a grand contribution to their adopted homelands. One bloody week in New York City, however, nearly erased the memory of this Irish heroism.

THE NEW YORK CITY
DRAFT RIOTS

Paddy McCarthy may or may not have been opposed to slavery or, for that matter, the Civil War. However, when bloody riots descended on New York City in July of 1863, Paddy helped save the city's most vulnerable citizens. When all was said and done, more than 100 people (mostly Irish) were officially dead. Hundreds more probably perished in what came to be called the New York City Draft Riots.

They began on the morning of July 13 when lists were posted naming men who had been drafted into the Union army to fight the Civil War. However, many Irish laborers were neutral on the war question. They were Democrats loyal to the Irish-dominated political machine known as Tammany Hall and, thus, skeptical of Republicans such as wartime president Abraham Lincoln. Some immigrants even opposed the war, fearing that if African-American slaves in the South were liberated, they might head north and take Irish jobs. The final straw, though, was that a draftee could buy

PROVOST GUARD ATTACKING THE RIOTER'S

his way out of the draft for $300. The rich were exempt, while poor immigrants were forced to fight.

That terrible July morning, mobs of mostly Irish (and some German) workers began looting stores and setting fires. Matters grew uglier when the rioters targeted African-American institutions. Paddy McCarthy, however, defied many of his angry countrymen and helped escort 200 African-American children from a "colored orphanage," which bloodthirsty rioters had targeted. After days of violence, peace was finally secured by troops returning from Gettysburg—as well as by quite a few Irish police officers.

To the Protestant middle classes, the riots proved that the Irish were violent brutes. "Stalwart young vixens and withered old hags were swarming everywhere, all cursing the 'bloody draft' and egging on their men," wrote anti-Irish diarist George Templeton Strong. "[T]he atrocities these Celtic devils perpetrated can hardly be paralleled in the history of human cruelty." Strong, of course, ignored heroes like Paddy McCarthy.

1865–1922
AT HOME, WORK, SCHOOL

UPWARDLY MOBILE

Father Woldron, a priest at St. John's parish in Chicago's heavily Irish South Side, did not like what he saw happening in the 1880s. He watched "in sorrow as hundreds of beloved families surrendered their humble homes and moved in affluence." Many of Chicago's Irish immigrants had finally earned enough money to leave the South Side tenements and slums and move to more fashionable neighborhoods, such as Englewood. There (much to the dismay of local Protestants) they laid foundations for working- or middle-class parishes such as St. Bernard's.

RIGHT: ...and then, having made his fortune, "homeward bound" for Dublin.

LEFT: Two lithographs by Joseph Keppler in Puck magazine show, first, a tattered Irishman "outward bound" and headed for New York...

Across America, in the decades following the Civil War, the Irish finally began leaving the shanty colonies they had haphazardly erected during the harsh famine years. From neat row houses in Baltimore to modest spired homes outside the factories of Bethlehem, Pennsylvania, the Irish were climbing toward the American middle class. As the Irish left the ghettos, Italian, Polish, and Jewish immigrants frequently moved in—just as the Irish had previously replaced working-class, native-born Protestants. (In fact, the Irish who

50

remained in the neighborhoods often sneered at the newcomers, just as earlier Irish immigrants had been looked down upon.)

By the end of the nineteenth century, the large majority of Irish Americans were still manual laborers. For a variety of reasons, though—unions, political ties, an affinity for police and firefighter work—many Irish were now putting abject poverty behind them. Many also credited their strong Irish-Catholic faith for creating a moral foundation that helped first-generation Irish avoid the worst temptations of slum life.

ABOVE: *Once they settled in U.S. cities, many Irish immigrant men gravitated toward the police force. Law enforcement provided a stable income as well as respect.*

LEFT: *Jacob Riis captured this image in a New York pub in the 1890s. Such saloons were a place where Irish immigrants could discuss politics, hold union meetings, and hear about job openings.*

Some Irish were even becoming fabulously wealthy. John Cudahy, a famine immigrant, built an ornate castle on Chicago's South Michigan Avenue. He had made a fortune in meatpacking, along with his brothers Patrick and Michael. James Augustine Farrell, meanwhile, born to immigrants in 1863, went on to become president of the U.S. Steel Corporation. That same year, Cork immigrant William Ford had a son, Henry, in Dearborn, Michigan, who would go to revolutionize the automobile industry.

Most Irish, however, were working class in 1900. Nearly 20 percent of America's Irish at that time were coachmen or drivers, and more than 10 percent were police officers or long-shoremen. Exceptional young men aspired to the law or politics, though it was well known that many Irish mothers had a soft spot for the priesthood. Women had fewer options. More and more daughters of hardworking domestic servants were becoming teachers, who would eventually dominate the big-city school systems. As a result, young Irish men and women were now meeting at, say, a formal dance sponsored by a local Ancient Order of Hibernians division rather than on board a cramped ship.

In Irish-American homes there never was a great tradition of immigrant cuisine. The Irish contribution to American tastebuds would come through local pubs or saloons—though not necessarily because of the Irish stereotype about drink. Not only were Irish-owned pubs a place for politics, union meetings, and camaraderie, many also served up hearty food at low prices, or even free, with a beer (favorites included corned beef and cabbage). This was a perfect menu for working men such as Patrick O'Callaghan. In an 1886 letter to his sister in Waterford, O'Callaghan—a Philadelphia iron-worker—touched on a number of key factors that helped the Irish leave the slums behind:

["Our brother] Owen and I were working at the locomotive works for $1.30 per day. We liked the work, but now our union is on strike against work reductions. Of 3,000 hands in this factory, nearly all Irish, there's only 500 still working. . . . We'll take any sort of job or starve sooner than submit. However there can be little fear for us as long as we stick together. There's a lot of Waterford people here, and every day we see people from the old country. Last night the Walshes visited our boarding house, and we drank, sang, and told stories 'til midnight. On St. Patrick's Day we had a grand parade and that night we had a great Waterford ball at which all the boys and girls danced just like home. Each for himself but all for one another is the way we get along. We've joined the Co. Waterford Society and the Ancient Order of Hibernians, which is established all over the country. As you see, Irishmen are well organized here under the principles of brotherly love and Christian charity."

BELOW: *Henry Ford, the son of an Irish immigrant who had settled in Michigan, later went on to revolutionize the automobile industry.*

RIGHT: *The Ford family is a classic story of immigrant success. Henry's portrait (right) appears prominently over Henry Ford II (standing) and his brothers Benson and William, all of whom went into the family business.*

As the twentieth century approached, the Irish were far from affluent. Many were still laying railroad tracks on the plains and digging sewer holes in the cities. Furthermore, the Irish could not leave certain stereotypes behind. In the late 1870s, July in New York always brought violence when Irish Protestants and Irish Catholics clashed during competing parades, which commemorated events in Ireland nearly two centuries old. From these pitched battles in the streets came the Orange Riots (orange being the traditional color of Protestants), which left dozens dead, hundreds injured, and supported the stereotype that the Irish were a genetically violent people. What tended to be forgotten was that the rioters, more often than not, were arrested by Irish police officers and might even be taken to be sentenced before an Irish judge.

After a day's work, lawmen—from the streets, as well as from the courts—might head to the saloon for a glass of beer before going home to their wives and children. Such people generally did not make the newspapers, but, increasingly, they formed the backbone of many major American cities from coast to coast.

TOP LEFT: *As Irish immigrants gained leadership posts in big city police departments, they entered the American middle class.*

FAR LEFT: *More and more Irish emigrating to America meant grander St. Patrick's Day parades, such as depicted in this illustration from 1874.*

RIGHT: *Violence, such as the Orange Riots of the 1870s, supported the stereotype that Irish Americans were genetically inclined to violence and disorder.*

THE ATTACK ON THE PROCESSION, ON EIGHTH AVENUE, BETWEEN TWENTY-FOURTH AND TWENTY-FIFTH STREETS.—From a Sketch by our Special Artist.—[See Page 605.]

BUILDING THE SCHOOLHOUSE

New York archbishop John Hughes set off a cultural war during the 1840s when he called America's public school system deeply anti-Catholic.

Hughes demanded that since native-born children received free education (with a decidedly Protestant tilt), Irish-Catholic immigrants should also receive government money to set up their own schools. Instead, New York educators begrudgingly toned down or neutralized religious content in the classroom. Still, Hughes and other Catholic leaders in the United States believed it was critical that Irish immigrants attend Catholic schools. "We have to build the schoolhouse first and the church afterward," Hughes said.

These poor immigrants thus laid the foundation for the sprawling Catholic school system in America. Facilities ranging from parish grade schools to prestigious higher learning institutions (such as Loyola University, Notre Dame, and Boston College) would help the Irish make the transition from the railroads and canals to Wall Street. Catholic schools did not merely educate. They also strengthened parish ties, with Irish children attending the same schools and church until they were at least 18 years old. Catholic Youth Organization (CYO) leagues, bingo nights, church socials—even dating—often revolved solely around parish environs and its parishioners. Hence, this explains the reason so many Irish Americans, when asked where they lived, responded by naming their parish rather than their geographical neighborhood.

Some memories of America's Irish-built Catholic schools are not, of course, so favorable—uncomfortable uniforms, raps on the knuckles, strict brothers and nuns. Yet, in the long

1927.

LEFT: *John (circled, right) and Joseph (left) Kennedy, in a 1927 photograph taken while the brothers attended Dexter, their school in Brookline, Massachusetts.*

run, historians such as Maureen Fitzgerald point out that Irish nuns in Catholic schools played as large a role in securing stability for poor immigrants as Irish politicians did.

To this day, Catholic schools remain attractive to Irish Americans, from blue-collar workers to artists. "Twenty years ago no one could have convinced me that I would send my children to Catholic schools," best-selling novelist Alice McDermott said recently, "but of course, that's where they are now."

ABOVE: *Catholic universities such as Loyola helped Irish Americans enter the middle class in America while maintaining close ties to their traditional faith.*

LEFT: *Irish nuns played an integral, though often unheralded role, in educating generations of Irish-American children in tight-knit parishes.*

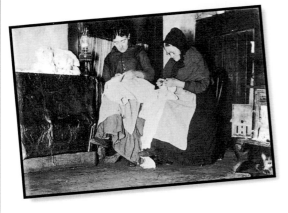

WANTED: YOUNG IRISH GIRL

On November 28, 1891, Mr. T. F. Green went to the New York Labor Exchange and, for a $2 fee, hired himself a domestic servant named Annie O'Brien. Annie, hired for $8 a month, then paid the agency $1 for finding her the work. Annie was only doing what Irish women had been doing for 50 years. Back in 1855, 75 percent of New York's 24,000 domestic servants were Irish. That number would not change much for decades. So many Irish

girls became domestics (almost always in upper-middle-class Protestant homes) that they were often called Bridget, regardless of their true names.

Unlike most other immigrant groups, more Irish women than men actually came to the United States. At the very least, a boy in Ireland might inherit a piece of land, not so for an Irish girl. Many immigrant women worked in factories as seamstresses; others became nurses in the fledgling Catholic hospitals system. However, the vast majority of Irish women became domestics, often working from 6 A.M. until midnight.

Still, the work gave Irish women a level of economic independence. They could send money or tickets to relatives in Ireland or contribute to church funds. As an alternative, Laois (pronounced "Leesh") native Julia Lough joined her four sisters in Connecticut to run their own dress shop. Three years later, she sold it to another Irish immigrant, Thomas McCarthy—with whom she ultimately had six children.

What with housework, domestic work, and child-rearing, life for Irish immigrant women could be excruciating. They are simultaneously credited with maintaining clean, pious, orderly homes amid adversity. In fact, Irish motherly sacrifice became such a noble ideal that it would be celebrated in tear-jerking songs such as "Mother Machree" (*above right*).

LEFT: *From New York (above, as depicted in this 1890 Jacob Riis photo) to South Carolina, Irish women held grueling jobs in factories and textile mills at the start of the twentieth century.*

BELOW: *Irish women often found nursing work in Catholic hospitals and dominated domestic service. Such servants were often referred to as "Bridget," regardless of their actual name.*

"Sure, I love the dear silver that shines in your hair,

And the brow that's all furrowed and wrinkled with care.

I kiss the dear fingers so toilworn for me.

Oh, God bless you and keep you, Mother Machree."

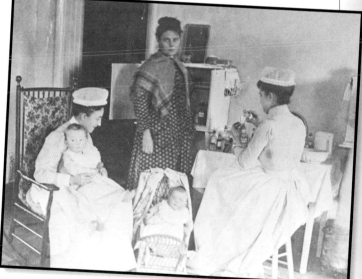

ON THE JOB

PADDY ON THE RAILWAY

Immigrants did much of the digging and heavy lifting along the Erie Canal, as well as mining up and down the East Coast in the 1830s and 1840s. After the Civil War, however, there was still much work to be done, particularly on America's rapidly expanding railroads. Once again, Irish immigrants—who did not settle in the great northeastern cities—were up to the task.

Many Irish by then held positions of authority with the railroad companies, such as James Harvey Strobridge, a close associate of Central Pacific Railroad owner Charles Crocker. In 1862, Crocker's company, along with Union Pacific, was authorized by Congress to build America's first

> **TRADITIONAL SONG**
>
> *"I'm weary of the railway*
> *Poor Paddy works on the Railway."*

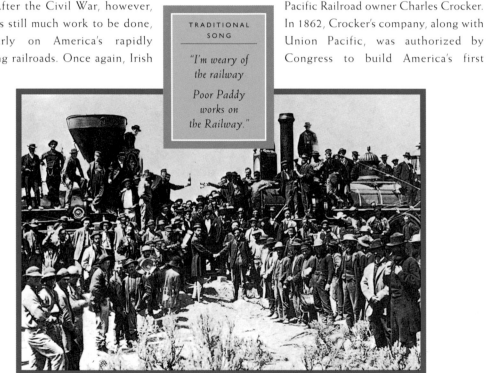

Fittingly, Anaconda was owned by County Cavan immigrant Marcus Daly, who had started his own western journey as a mere miner and foreman.

Irish immigrants like Daly built lives quite different from their counterparts back east—though there were similarities. San Francisco's political machine helped propel Irish immigrants to U.S. Senate seats in 1861 and 1868. Frank McCoppin became San Francisco's mayor in 1867, more than a decade before Boston or New York elected an Irish mayor. Roscommon native John G. Downey even became California governor in 1860. East or west, the Irish always knew the importance of politics.

transcontinental railroad. Working alongside Chinese laborers, Irish immigrants built the first coast-to-coast railroad line, laying track at an astonishing rate—once setting down ten miles of track in a single day. The harsh work and low pay made tunes such as "Poor Paddy Works on the Railway" popular among the men.

In search of better pay for easier work, many Irish went west after the gold rush of 1849. Irish immigrants John Mackay and James Fair started out as Nevada miners and ultimately made a fortune through their investments. Of course, most Irish in the West toiled for more modest wages. Many were attracted to the copper mines of Butte, Montana, where workers at the Anaconda Mine gathered to live in what came to be called Dublin Gulch.

LEFT: *Irish laborers were prominent among those who gathered to commemorate the completion of the Transcontinental railroad in Promontory, Utah in 1869.*

RIGHT: *The Gold Rush in Nevada and other Western states provided opportunities for Irish immigrants that were not always available in the Eastern United States.*

THE KNIGHTS OF LABOR

"Pray for the dead and fight like hell for the living." So roared one of the more unlikely labor leaders of nineteenth-century America, Mary Harris "Mother" Jones, just one of thousands of Irish who built a towering union tradition in the United States. Born to a poor Cork family, Mother Jones's grandfather was hanged by the British as a traitor, and her father was forced to flee for defying British rule. So activism was in her blood. After losing her husband and children to a yellow fever epidemic, she criss-crossed America in the latter half of the nineteenth century, agitating for workers' rights, until she died in her nineties. Her successor, in many ways, was Elizabeth Gurley Flynn, a dedicated Marxist whose commitment to both communism and workers landed her in prison twice. Out west, Kate Kennedy and in the east Kate Mullaney were other notable Irish-born women who became labor leaders.

Meanwhile, one of the largest American labor unions ever, the Knights of Labor, was led by Terrence Powderly, the son of immigrants. By 1886, Powderly led as many as 700,000 Knights nationwide, winning key strikes against business magnates such as Jay Gould. The Knights were also noteworthy because they organized women as well as African Americans.

ABOVE: *Mary Harris "Mother" Jones became one of America's most powerful labor leaders.*

RIGHT: *Elizabeth Gurley Flynn was an influential Irish-American labor leader who espoused controversial views.*

FAR RIGHT: *In the 1950s, George Meaney was the leader of the American Federation of Labor (AFL).*

One of the most notorious labor episodes in American history unfolded in Pennsylvania's coal region. In the 1860s, Irish miners formed a union to counter the harsh policies of the Philadelphia & Reading Railroad. A faction within the union, calling itself the Mollie Maguires, used intimidation and even violence to pressure management. Twenty alleged Mollies were ultimately hanged in 1877, based on what is now believed to be flimsy evidence. Right into the twentieth century, the Irish remained prominent labor leaders. Bronx-born George Meany became president of the mammoth AFL in 1952. John Sweeney, the son of immigrants from Leitrim, led the AFL-CIO (American Federation of Labor/Congress of Industrial Organizations) into the twenty-first century.

POLITICS

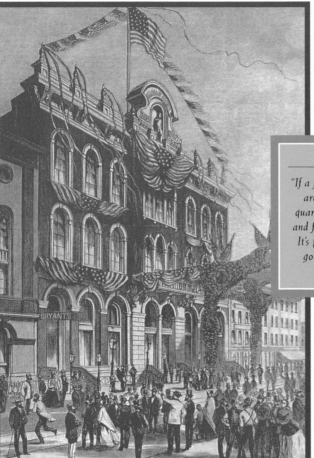

LEFT: *In 1868, the new Tammany Hall building—home to New York City's infamous Democratic political organization—was unveiled. For more than a century the Irish were key Tammany Hall members.*

GEORGE WASHINGTON PLUNKITT

"If a family is burned out I don't ask whether they are Republicans or Democrats . . . I just get quarters for them if their clothes were burned up, and fix them up til they get things runnin' again. It's philanthropy, but it's politics, too—mighty good politics. Who can tell how many votes one of these fires brings me?"

FAR RIGHT: *This Thomas Nast cartoon depicts key constituencies of the U.S. Democratic Party. They include (at left) an apelike Irishman with a club, and a reference to the "Five Points" neighborhood on his hat. All are depicted as suppressing the rights of African Americans.*

TAMMANY HALL

This is the world according to George Washington Plunkitt (*see box left*). The son of Irish immigrants, Plunkitt rose through the ranks of New York's Democratic Party. In 1905, he wrote *Plunkitt of Tammany Hall*, the title of which refers to the most (in)famous of America's many Irish-dominated political machines.

Going back to the years just after the Revolutionary War, America's two main political factions had clear positions on the Irish. In the 1790s, the Federalist Party favored the Alien and Sedition Acts, aimed mainly at deporting French and Irish Catholics, both of which groups heavily supported the rival Democratic Party. When the Irish Famine struck, Tammany Hall's New York Democrats saw thousands of potential votes in the desperate immigrants. Legend has it that immigrants would go straight from the boat to a Tammany court with notes reading, "Please naturalize the bearer."

Eventually, cities from Boston to San Francisco had massive political organizations dominated by Irishmen such as Daniel O'Connell (Albany) and Tom Pendergast (Kansas City). Why did the Irish perform so well at politics? Unlike earlier German immigrants and later Italians and Jews, the Irish knew America's language. Furthermore, throughout the nineteenth and twentieth centuries, the Irish kept coming to America in large numbers.

Machine Democrats offered continued assistance in exchange for political support. Political machines, of course, were often terribly corrupt, stealing millions from the pockets of taxpayers. Construction jobs that should have cost about $1 million ended up costing $5 million by the time all the machine pockets were lined. Worse, the finished jobs could often be dangerously shoddy.

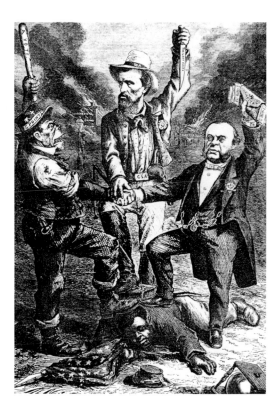

Big-city machines eventually went too far, even by their own lofty standards of criminal excess. San Francisco boss Chris Buckley was indicted in 1891 on bribery charges, while Kansas City's Tom Pendergast spent 15 months in prison on tax charges in the late 1930s. New York boss William Marcy Tweed (a non-Irish Protestant who clearly believed that power and money could transcend ethnic differences) was also jailed in the 1870s.

Sixty years later, facing a slew of charges, Mayor Jimmy Walker actually fled New York, essentially drawing the curtain on Tammany's heyday.

However, elite, antimachine reformers were not always driven by the noble goal of exposing political crime. There remained a strong whiff of anti-Irish bigotry in the political cartoons of Thomas Nast and even in the mainstream press. When Tammany Hall was thrown out of power in 1872 (the Democrats would return, of course), the *New York Times* sneered that New York City would no longer be "tyrannized over by our esteemed friends from the Emerald Isle.

LEFT: *New York Mayor Jimmy Walker became a symbol of the Roaring Twenties, and of Tammany Hall corruption. Facing charges, he fled America with his showgirl mistress.*

This is going to be an American City once more—not simply a large kind of Dublin."

Such opinions failed to acknowledge the roots of machine support in impoverished tenements. More importantly, though, some machine politicians were actually able to eschew corruption. Harry Truman, of Kansas City, was one such. Another was a New York lawmaker named Al Smith, who would become the first Irish Catholic from a major political party to run for president in 1928. This, however, was no moment of triumph for the Irish. Smith's own background—political, ethnic, and religious—would lead to a dark moment in American history.

LEFT: *Mayor Richard J. Daley ruled Chicago politics for over 20 years, and became such a powerful national figure he was known as a "president maker."*

RIGHT: *Mayor Daley played a particularly important—and controversial—role in the election of America's first Irish-Catholic president. Here, John F. Kennedy posed with Daley and his family in the Oval Office in 1961.*

FAR RIGHT: *Another powerful Irish-American mayor was Jersey City's Frank Hague. Though he's seen here campaigning with Franklin Delano Roosevelt in 1932, FDR secretly loathed the abrasive Hague, who was famous for proclaiming "I am the Law."*

CITY HALL

Going back to 1683, when the Duke of York selected Irish-born Protestant Thomas Dongan as colonial governor of New York, sons of the Emerald Isle held powerful political positions in the New World. Not until two centuries later, though, following the establishment of Irish Catholic-dominated political machines, would Irish immigrants win leadership posts in the big cities. The 1880s saw the election of Irish mayors in New York (William Grace, born in County Cork) and Boston (Hugh O'Brien, born in Fermanagh). For the next 70 years, Irish mayors would dominate the big cities, from Jersey City to New Orleans. Below are some of the most memorable.

Perhaps the most powerful Irish-American mayor ever was Chicago's Richard Daley, who ran the town for more than 20 years, beginning with his 1955 election. More interested in power and influence than in lining his pockets, Daley was a humble, devout Catholic who raised his family not far from the South Side Irish ghetto where he grew up. A multiethnic town, Chicago required a mayor who knew how to reward all ethnic groups, even African Americans, whom Daley relied on for delivering votes in segregated African-American neighborhoods. Daley became such a key figure in the Democratic Party that he was known as a "president maker," whose support was needed to nominate any White House candidate. His image

was tarnished by the violent events of the 1968 Chicago Democratic convention. In the election before he died in office in 1976, though, Daley received nearly 60 percent of the vote. Fittingly, his son Richard was later elected Chicago mayor.

Born in a Jersey City tenement to immigrants from Cavan, Frank Hague helped build a political machine that elected him mayor in 1917 and made him New Jersey's most powerful politician. Famous for proclaiming "I am the Law," Hague ruled Jersey City from 1917 to 1947. Though he was voted out, then reelected (and later jailed), Hague remained so powerful for decades that even President Franklin Roosevelt, who loathed him, could not rid Hague from the party's ranks.

Possibly the Irish mayor who most proudly flaunted his rascality was James Michael Curley, the son of Connemara immigrants born in South Boston. Between 1914 and 1949, Curley was elected and then thrown out of office more often (four times) than he was thrown into jail (twice). He enjoyed baiting Boston's Protestant elite, much to the glee of Irish-Catholic voters. He also loved to have fun with rumors of voter fraud, saying, "Vote early and often for Curley." Edwin O'Connor's famous novel *The Last Hurrah* (made into a movie starring Spencer Tracy) was a thinly veiled chronicle of Curley's final race.

David Lawrence, the father of the Pittsburgh renaissance, ruled the Steel City from 1946 to

ABOVE AND LEFT: *Boston's James Michael Curley was elected mayor four times. He was embraced by many working-class Boston Irish, and despised by the city's Yankee Protestant establishment. Curley was also jailed twice, and loved to poke fun at charges of voter fraud by saying: "Vote early and often for Curley."*

1959. Before his election, Pittsburgh was a smog-choked city regularly beset by floods. Lawrence not only cleaned up the city's streets and air but also brought Pittsburgh's moribund economy into the twentieth century. He was almost a caricature of the stage Irishman, who loved to tell "Irish and Catholic stories as if he were straight off the boat from County Mayo," according to one reporter.

Detroit's Frank Murphy was one of the few mayors to go on to bigger and better things. At the height of the Great Depression, Murphy steered Detroit through hunger and bankruptcy. He later became Michigan governor and U.S. attorney general in 1939, and he was finally appointed to the U.S. Supreme Court. Murphy was one of the few Irish mayors to defy Curley's bon mot, "Being Mayor is great, but there's no future in it."

ABOVE: *Irish-American writer Edwin O'Connor based his famous book* The Last Hurrah *on James Michael Curley's final run for mayor.*

RIGHT: *Detroit's Frank Murphy was one of a few Irish-American mayors who went on to bigger things, later serving as governor, U.S. attorney general, and U.S. Supreme Court justice.*

RIGHT: *John Francis "HoneyFitz" Fitzgerald was a political and social trailblazer in Boston. Here, he joins some of son-in-law Joseph P. Kennedy's children as they all set sail for Britain, where Joe Kennedy served as Ambassador from 1938 to 1940.*

KENNEDY AND FITZGERALD OF BOSTON

It is ironic, of course, that no American city is so thoroughly Irish and Catholic as Boston. This is the city, after all, that nurtured the wealthy Protestant elite who had fought a successful revolution against the "mother country" (England, of course). Following the Irish Famine, though, the Catholic and Protestant communities would forever be at odds. At no place was this more evident than in the voting booth. Two wealthy, powerful men are perhaps more responsible than any others for promoting Irish-Catholic politics in Boston.

John Francis Fitzgerald was a trailblazer even before he became the first American-born child of Irish immigrants to become Boston's mayor in 1909. HoneyFitz, as he was known, was the first Irish Catholic to study at the elite Boston Latin School. He was elected to several political offices (as a Democrat, of course). However, a squabble with fellow Irish bosses led to the mayoral election

LEFT: *The Kennedy family in Boston, 1934. Joseph P. Kennedy and Rose Fitzgerald Kennedy built a political dynasty, but also one that endured great personal tragedy.*

of a Republican in 1907. When finally elected Boston mayor, HoneyFitz was a passionate defender of the town's working-class Irish, much to the dismay of Boston's Yankee elite.

HoneyFitz and his wife Josephine Hannon raised their six children comfortably, including their daughter Rose, who would help create Boston's other prominent political family. Rose's husband was Joseph Patrick Kennedy, a Harvard graduate and millionaire. Kennedy, however— always tainted by his past—would never be elected to public office. Aside from whispers that he made money as a bootlegger during Prohibition, Kennedy spent the late 1930s arguing that America should stay out of World War II and, instead, should negotiate with Hitler. So he worked behind the scenes. As a fundraiser for Franklin Roosevelt, Kennedy gained access to all the right people and laid the groundwork for his four sons. Perhaps one of them might become the first Irish-Catholic resident of the home that Joe—for all his money— would never inhabit: the White House.

AL SMITH

Eight-year-old Edith Garret wore her Al Smith campaign button proudly. However, her parents warned her, "They'll never let him get elected because he's Catholic."

Smith, running for president in 1928, won big in the Garrets' heavily Irish West Side Manhattan district, with 13,950 votes to Herbert Hoover's 4,077. Across America, though, Smith was trounced in an election that saw the anti-Catholic Ku Klux Klan play a major role. It was a dark moment in U.S. history.

RIGHT: *New York Governor Al Smith, born on Manhattan's Lower East Side, was the first Roman Catholic to run for president as a major party candidate.*

Al Smith was born on Manhattan's bustling Lower East Side in 1873. His paternal grandparents were born in Germany and Italy; his maternal relatives were all Irish. Raised by his mother, Smith thought of himself as Irish, and New Yorkers saw him that way. Like many an Irish politician before him, he was a Tammany Democrat loyal to the working class. After serving as one of New York's most popular governors, he was ready to ask the question, "Would Americans elect a Catholic president?"

On September 19, 1928, Al Smith got his answer. As his campaign train entered Oklahoma, the KKK burned crosses. Enemies—many within

LEFT: Smith was wildly popular in New York, particularly among immigrants and their children. A ticker tape parade was thrown in Smith's honor when he launched his run for the presidency in 1928.

BELOW: Smith, however, faced a brutal campaign. The rabidly anti-Catholic, anti-immigrant Ku Klux Klan burned crosses at certain Smith campaign appearances.

his own Democratic Party—linked Smith to the Irish stereotypes of "rum, Romanism, and rebellion." Amid dire warnings that he would be loyal to the pope, not America, Smith lost even his beloved home state of New York.

Perhaps his candidacy was doomed from the start. The economy was booming in 1928. Many in the American heartland were turned off by his thick New York accent. Though Smith himself was incorruptible, he was linked to the infamous Tammany machine. Later, when the Great Depression struck during the early 1930s, many would credit Smith's popularity among big-city ethnic voters with helping to elect Franklin Roosevelt on a New Deal plank. Smith, however, never recovered from that awful 1928 campaign. As little Edith Garret's parents knew, Irish Catholics had come far by 1928—but they still had a considerable way to go.

SAINTS AND SINNERS

THE BRAVEST AND THE FINEST

Matthew T. Brennan, who was raised in New York's Five Points slum, joined the city's volunteer fire department in the early 1840s and was eventually elected company foreman. Given the extraordinary role that firehouses played in nineteenth-century New York, this was a plum position. Firefighters were colorful heroes and were worshipped by street gangs and politicians alike. In fact, Brennan went on to become one of the first Irish Catholics to run for a statewide office. He did not win that race but did go on to hold citywide office and become a Tammany Hall power broker.

Brennan's career suggests both the prominence of firehouses in America's big cities and the way

LEFT: *The New York Fire Department has always had a strong Irish tradition. Roughly 30 percent were Irish-born, according to an 1888 survey.*

in which the Irish used civil service work to advance in America. In no city was that more clearly evident than in New York. Before the famine years, few firefighters—or police officers—were Irish. In fact, many poor Irish immigrants despised the police, with whom they often clashed in the slums. By 1855, though, 17 percent of New York's volunteer fire department were Irish-born. With firehouses and police precincts intimately tied to local political machines, civil service jobs helped the Irish to achieve stability.

An 1888 list of 1,000 Fire Department of New York (FDNY) employees showed nearly 300 born in Ireland, according to author Terry Golway. Irish names accounted for nearly 75 percent of the department. Similarly, a mid-1880s survey showed that one-third of the 3,000 New York police officers were Irish-born. Among them was famine immigrant Thomas Byrnes, who came to America at six years old and later enlisted in the Union army. In 1880, he took over the New York Police Department's (NYPD's) Detective Bureau. His success in solving crimes astonished the public, who kept up with "the great detective" in newspaper stories. In fact, Byrnes—who loved the attention—was so confident of his skills that he dared Jack the Ripper to come to New York, as the killer was terrorizing London in the 1880s.

LUDLOW FIRE DEPARTMENT.   PHOTO BY MC MANUS, LUDLOW.

ABOVE: *Though firefighters, with their red trucks and daring jobs, were seen as folk heroes, many Irish Americans were simply attracted to the job's stability and benefits.*

RIGHT: *Another reason the Irish excelled in police and fire departments was because politics played a key role in all hiring and promotions. Fire chiefs such as T.J. O'Connor (right) had many friends among Irish political leaders.*

The list of names of NYPD commissioners reads like an Ancient Order of Hibernians (AOH) division membership list: Kennedy, Kelly, O'Ryan, O'Brien, Maguire, and three different Murphys. The Irish Mafia, as the NYPD came to be known, always knew that with their jobs' stability and benefits came risks. Irish families who sent sons (and increasingly daughters) onto tough streets always dreaded the phone call that might reveal that a loved one was injured or killed in the line of duty. Despite the danger, however, civil service jobs continue to beckon Irish families such as the Bresnans.

TOP: *The heavily Irish Fire Department of New York has become a symbol of heroism around the world.*

RIGHT: *Efforts to bring more women into American fire departments have been mixed, though this Washington D.C. fire company already had a Ladies Auxiliary in 1928.*

FAR RIGHT: *On September 11, 2001, a disproportionate number of Irish-American police officers and firefighters were among those who perished.*

Young John Bresnan's family left Ireland in 1844, settling in New York's 6th Ward. He joined Engine 21 as a volunteer in 1861 and went on to become one of the department's most influential leaders. On a freezing night in December 1894, Bresnan was killed after a water tower collapsed during a fire. The city mourned, while Bresnan's now parentless children went to live with relatives. John Bresnan Jr. eventually joined the FDNY, as did two of his sons—one of whom would have been on duty during the terrorist attacks on September 11 had he not retired two months earlier. A third Bresnan son did not go into the family business; instead, he joined the NYPD.

Irish names were particularly prominent among the 343 firefighters and 23 police officers who died on September 11, 2001 (dozens of *claddagh* rings were subsequently found in the World Trade Center wreckage). For months afterward, the mournful wail of Irish bagpipes could be heard at funeral services throughout the region for New York's bravest and finest.

IRISH GANGSTERS

ABOVE: *Jacob Riis captured this image from Mulberry Street in Manhattan, a notorious meeting point for gangsters and criminals from all ethnic backgrounds.*

As the seven gangsters who assembled in a Chicago alley on February 14, 1929 illustrate, not all Irish Americans joined the civil service. Many joined criminal gangs. During that St. Valentine's Day massacre, Al Capone's killers were gunning for Irish gangster George "Bugs" Moran. However, the disciple of slain Irish boss Deanie O'Banion was not among the seven thugs executed by Capone. Still, Moran's empire was crippled, ending flush years for the Irish mob in Chicago.

Going back to the famine years, Irish gangs did battle with anti-Irish-American gangs in most cities where immigrants settled. Members of Chicago's Ragen's Colts liked to boast, "Hit me and you hit two thousand." In St. Louis, Egan's Rats stuffed ballot boxes and intimidated voters to advance favored political figures.

With the advent of Prohibition in 1919, Irish criminals were among the many ethnic gangsters who made a fortune selling illegal booze. Chicago was probably the center of Irish organized crime, much to the dismay of Italian-American criminals such as Al Capone, who had Deanie O'Banion killed in 1924 and Bugs Moran neutralized by 1929.

During the 1930s, New York's West Side (especially the neighborhood of Hell's Kitchen) was Irish turf ruled by the Gophers, headed by Owney "the Killer" Madden. Madden flourished because he was willing to cooperate with Italian and Jewish

HELL'S
KITCHEN
THATS US
WHATS THE USE
WE'RE GOING
TO COOK
THAT KAISER'S GOOSE
GOPHERS

gangsters. County Kildare-born Vincent "Mad Dog" Coll began his criminal career similarly, as a hitman for Dutch Schultz, but his demise came when he wanted more money and muscle for himself. Even Owney Madden was among those who collaborated in the 1932 hit that left Coll dead on the floor of a West 23rd Street drugstore.

The Westies Irish gang would rule Hell's Kitchen for decades more, whereas Boston's "Whitey" Bulger ruled an Irish empire into the 1980s and 1990s. Still on the FBI's most wanted list, Bulger vanished and has yet to be captured.

ABOVE: *George "Bugs" Moran (left, along with lawyer George Bieber) was one of Chicago's most infamous Irish gangsters.*

WAR

THE EASTER RISING AND AFTER

The day after Easter Sunday 1916, a ragtag bunch of 150 Irish rebels seized Dublin's General Post Office. Led by James Connolly and Padraic Pearse, the rebels took down Britain's Union Jack flag, raised the Irish tricolor, and issued their own declaration of independence—known as the Easter Proclamation. It demanded an end to British rule in Ireland.

The Easter Rising marked the beginning of a turbulent decade of war in Ireland. Two years earlier, of course, Europe had exploded into World War I. Bloodshed of unprecedented proportions soaked the fields of France as French and British soldiers battled the Germans. In fact, the war so preoccupied British leaders that a fledgling movement for Irish independence was abruptly halted. So, in 1916, the rebels took matters into their own hands.

The Easter Rising was the culmination of decades of support for Irish rebellion, not just in Ireland but in the United States as well. Throughout the late nineteenth century, exiles such as John Devoy rallied advocates for a free Ireland, raising millions of dollars for the cause.

In Ireland, however, support for the Easter rebels was fairly weak; that is, until the British authorities responded. After shelling the GPO, leaving the middle of Dublin smoldering, they seized the rebels and condemned them to death in secret trials. A total of 15 Irish rebels were hanged, thus ensuring Pearse and Connolly a place in the annals of Irish martyrdom alongside Wolfe Tone and the heroes of the 1798 rebellion. Several rebels were spared and jailed, including New York-born Eamon De Valera (whose immigrant mother had married a Spaniard). Nevertheless, a new push for Irish independence had begun.

Across the Atlantic, meanwhile, anti-British sentiment among Irish Americans led many to oppose U.S. entrance into World War I. At the same time, President Woodrow Wilson criticized "hyphenated-Americans," whose homeland links tainted their view of U.S. policy. When the United States did

BELOW: *Following the 1916 Easter Rising in Dublin, crowds gathered outside Mount Joy prison to pray for rebels who had been sentenced to death by* British authorities. The Rising was not particularly popular among Irish citizens until the British executed several Irish rebels, turning them into martyrs.

ABOVE: *Dublin's Sackville Road Post Office lay in ruins following the Easter Rising.*

FAR LEFT: *Statue dedicated to Irish commander James Connolly, one of the leaders of the Easter Rising.*

enter the war in 1917, though, many brave Irish Americans enlisted. Fighting 69th sergeant Joyce Kilmer recruited "strong, intelligent, decent living men whose sturdy Americanism was strengthened and vivified by their Celtic blood." Reared on Civil War stories of Thomas Meagher and the 69th, Buffalo-born lawyer William J. "Wild Bill" Donovan was awarded the Medal of Honor.

With Germany defeated in 1918, many Irish Americans turned their attention to establishing an independent Ireland. Emerging as a key Irish leader was none other than Eamon De Valera. Jailed for the Easter Rebellion, he escaped with the help of fellow rebels Michael Collins and Harry Boland in 1919. By June, De Valera had gone to New York to raise $5 million for Irish freedom.

At the same time, violence raged in Ireland. It occurred in the north, where the Protestant majority in Ulster engaged in anti-Catholic pogroms. It also occurred in the south, where police forces known as the Black and Tans terrified local Catholics in search of a group now called the Irish Republican Army (IRA).

In response, the IRA, led by Michael Collins, initiated a new kind of war, using guerrilla tactics to attack secretly the more powerful British forces. In an attempt to end the violence in Ireland, the British finally offered Irish leaders such as Collins and De Valera a deal. Ireland's 26 southern counties would essentially rule themselves; however, the Protestant-dominated Ulster counties in the north would continue to remain under British rule.

Fatefully, in 1921, Collins accepted partition. De Valera and soldiers who were loyal to him rejected the deal, and an Irish Civil War broke out. Forces of what was now called the Irish Free State battled republicans, who eventually assassinated Michael Collins for accepting the deal with England. In the end, however, a war-weary Irish public—and even De Valera—accepted partition. After the Irish authorities hanged more than 70 dissident republicans, the Irish Free State entered a new era. In the north, however, Catholics remained second-class citizens, a situation that would lead to massive civil rights protests—and bloodshed—in the 1960s.

LEFT: *Ten thousand San Franciscans came out to see Irish leader—and prison escapee— Eamon De Valera in 1919 (center, the taller fellow with glasses).*

BELOW: *Michael Collins eventually got the British to the negotiating table, and agreed to a "partition" of Ireland. It led to his assassination in 1921.*

MUSIC AND SPORT

"THE PIPES ARE CALLING"

"Danny Boy" is perhaps the most beloved Irish song ever recorded. However, the song's mournful lyrics were actually penned by a British lawyer. This illustrates an important fact: while Irish immigrants brought an astonishingly rich tradition of music and dance to America, it was also a complicated tradition. Even before the famine, music in Ireland had undergone profound changes, with ancient Gaelic traditions giving way to more modern English ones. By the time the Irish came to America,

"Oh Danny Boy, the pipes, the pipes are calling . . ."

RIGHT: *Edwin Thomas Roberts' painting* The Overture *depicts an Irish musician performing on the uilleann pipes.*

which had its own rich musical tradition, new forms of Irish music were being born.

Ultimately, Irish music would diverge in two separate directions. Big-city Irish Catholics enjoyed rough, raucous songs about life in America or sentimental ballads about the old country. Lyrics might also be used for political purposes, in order to rally workers or rail against British injustice in Ireland. Instrumental music, meanwhile, would whip crowds into a dance frenzy at a *ceili* (KAY-lee, or group dancing, usually in a hall) or *seisiun* (se-SHOON, or informal music sessions, often in saloons). Rural Scotch-Irish Protestants, however, favored fiddle- and banjo-based music, which later evolved into hillbilly music and today's wildly popular country music.

Whatever form it took, Irish music sustained immigrants in America for generations. Instruments long favored by Irish musicians include the tin whistle, flute, and *uilleann* (ILL-in) pipes. Two additional staples of Irish music were mentioned by the *Boston Pilot* newspaper in July of 1846, reporting on Irish immigrants who gathered in "places of low resort, where the fiddle or the bag-pipes can be heard until 11 or 12 o'clock."

Throughout the nineteenth century, working-class Irish audiences also flocked to theaters, where song was among the main attractions. Frequently characters were "stage Irish"—whimsical leprechauns or drunken, apelike oafs. Some middle-class Irish were offended by these caricatures. However, many working-class theatergoers embraced the comical tunes, which reflected their rough-and-tumble urban lives.

By the late nineteenth century, record producers in New York's Tin Pan Alley district were using Americanized Irish music and lyrics to produce popular standards like "My Wild Irish Rose," "Mother Machree," and "When Irish Eyes Are Smiling." These songs still bring tears to the eyes of some and remain St. Patrick's Day

RIGHT: *Many of country music's biggest contemporary stars, such as Garth Brooks, owe their popularity to traditional music that had its roots in Ireland.*

LEFT: *The world-famous Chieftains (photographed under the Brooklyn Bridge in 2001) led a revival of Irish folk music during the 1960s.*

RIGHT: *Bing Crosby (seen with Frank Sinatra) was famous for playing a singing Irish priest in 1940s films. Crosby bridged the gap between sentimental Irish music and American popular music.*

BELOW RIGHT: *Gene Kelly was a famous Irish-American dancer who became wildly popular with mainstream U.S. audiences.*

favorites. The Irish-American songwriting duo of Harrigan and Hart produced dozens of these tunes. However, they also wrote insightful ones as well, such as "Muldoon the Solid Man," about a Donegal immigrant who becomes a generous politician in New York's 14th Ward. Also appealing—even to Irish Americans who had never been to the old country—were romantic songs of Ireland, such as J. K. Brennan's and Ernie Balls's "A Little Bit of Heaven." Whatever form it took, by 1892 the demand for Irish music in New York City was so strong that funds were raised to open Celtic Hall, a large song-and-dance venue.

In the twentieth century, Irish music continued to thrive in ethnic enclaves, at weddings, and even in the home, where St. Patrick's Day parties did not seem complete without a fiddle-playing uncle and an aunt who could still dance a fine jig. The Irish, however, were also as susceptible as the rest of America to popular American crooners such as Bing Crosby and Frank Sinatra. The former was Irish on his mother's side and would go on to become the famed singing Irish priest in 1940s films such as *Going My Way*. George M. Cohan and Gene Kelly were other Irish song-and-dance performers who moved from ethnic theater to the mainstream.

The 1960s brought a revival of traditional Irish music, led by The Chieftains, Tommy Makem, and The Clancy Brothers. To this day, Irish music remains popular, from the world-famous Irish Tenors and rock 'n' roll flash of Riverdance to informal pub sessions in the Bronx.

FOOTBALL
NOTRE DAME (SOUTH BEND) by
SOUTH·SHORE·LINE

Trains from Chicago Operated over Illinois Central Railroad from Randolph,
Van Buren, 12th, 43rd, 53rd, and 63rd St. Stations.

ABOVE: *The "Fighting Irish" of
Notre Dame continues to be
one of the most popular sports
teams in the United States.*

THE DIAMOND AND THE RING

When Irish sports fans talk about a hurling pitch, it has nothing to do with baseball. Simply put, Irish sports did not travel well to America. True, to this day crowds gather every Sunday at Gaelic Park in the Bronx, Chicago, or Boston. They watch hurling (a 2,000-year-old game that is similar to lacrosse; the field is referred to as a pitch) and Gaelic football (a kind of rugby/soccer, which is even older than hurling). These matches are all sanctioned by the Gaelic Athletic Association (GAA).

However, the vast majority of Irish in America thrived at sports native to the United States. Most famously are the Fighting Irish of Notre Dame. The heavily Irish football squads of the early twentieth century were always informally known by this name, though school officials did not sanction it until 1927.

In boxing, though, the Irish have had the largest impact. The son of immigrants, Boston-born pugilist John L. Sullivan was the most popular athlete of his era. Fellow Irish-American "Gentleman" Jim Corbett finally floored Sullivan in an epic 1892 bout, which went 21 rounds! Other Irish-American boxing greats include Jack Dempsey, Gene Tunney, and Gerry Cooney.

Baseball, too, proved attractive to Irish immigrants such as Cork-born pitcher Anthony Mullane, who won nearly 300 games pitching in the 1880s.

Baseball was also attractive to the American-born sons of immigrants, who lived in the big cities and followed local teams. Mike "King" Kelly was one of the late-nineteenth-century's most feared sluggers. Time has not been so kind to Irish baseball owners, however. Charlie Comiskey—the son of famine immigrants—was so famously stingy that his White Sox took money to throw the 1919 World Series. Walter O'Malley, meanwhile, infamously moved the Dodgers out of Brooklyn in 1958.

Diverse sporting stars can also claim Irish heritage. These include tennis great John McEnroe and golfer Ben Hogan (born in Dublin, Texas).

ABOVE: *Wildly popular Irish boxer John L. Sullivan fought in one of the last bare-knuckle matches ever. The Boston-born Sullivan finally beat Jack Kilrain in the 75th round during the 1889 bout. Fellow Irish-American boxer "Gentleman" Jim Corbett finally beat Sullivan in 1892.*

RIGHT: *Tennis great and New York native John McEnroe was among the most popular Irish-American athletes of his era.*

1922–1945
WRITERS AND ARTISTS

THE IRISH GO TO HOLLYWOOD

LEFT: *The notorious 1927 film* The Callahans and the Murphys *explored two rowdy tenement families. Irish-Catholic groups boycotted the film, and several cities banned it.*

From Jimmy Cagney to Ed Burns, Hollywood has always known it could turn to the Irish for a good movie. As far back as 1911, director Sidney Olcott made films with not-so-subtle titles such as *Ireland the Oppressed* and *Come Back to Erin*.

Perhaps the most important early Irish movie, however, was the notorious *The Callahans and the Murphys* (1927). Irish-Catholic social organizations were outraged at the film's depiction of two rowdy, gin-swilling tenement families who incessantly bless themselves and check their own bodies for lice. The film was even banned in several cities

LEFT: *Jimmy Cagney's portrayal of Irish gangster Tom Powers, in the 1931 classic* The Public Enemy, *electrified audiences.*

and contributed to calls for a code that Hollywood had to follow, to clean up movie content. The eventual result was the production code, which famously restricted the content of all Hollywood movies into the 1960s.

Also alarming many Americans in the 1930s was the popularity of gangster films. No actor was more explosive than New York-native Jimmy Cagney, playing Tom Powers in the 1931 classic *The Public Enemy*. Cagney was an Irish thug again in *Angels with Dirty Faces* in 1938, playing Rocky Sullivan, a neighborhood tough who is idolized by local kids. However, Rocky's childhood partner in crime (played by Pat O'Brien) is now a priest and pleads with Rocky: if he is not going to reform, at least make sure the kids do not go bad.

The most popular priest of Irish cinema, however, was Spencer Tracy's beloved Father Flanagan from *Boys Town* (1938), which was based on the saintly, real-life exploits of the Irish-born clergyman. The Irish priest would remain a Hollywood staple for decades, epitomized by Bing Crosby in both *Going My Way* (1944) and *The Bells of St. Mary's* (1945).

Jimmy Cagney, meanwhile, traded in his tommy gun for dancing shoes in the life story of George M. Cohan in the movie *Yankee Doodle Dandy* (1942). Prior to the famous scene in which Cohan tap-dances down the White House steps, President Franklin Roosevelt tells him, "That's one thing I've always admired about you

TOP TO BOTTOM: *Spencer Tracy played Father Flanagan in the classic Boys' Town; Pat O'Brien played a priest opposite Cagney in* Angels with Dirty Faces; *Marlon Brando brought poignancy to the role of a Brooklyn Irish dockworker in 1954's* On the Waterfront.

ABOVE: *Spencer Tracy plays an old-time Boston politician making one last run for office in* The Last Hurrah, *based in part on Boston mayor James Michael Curley.*

RIGHT: *Scarlett O'Hara was not merely a spoiled southern belle in* Gone With the Wind—*she was also the daughter of an Irish immigrant.*

Irish Americans. You carry your love of country like a flag, right out in the open."

In 1945, the tenements of the Callahans and the Murphys were handled much more poignantly by director Elia Kazan in his classic melodrama *A Tree Grows in Brooklyn*. Nine years later, Kazan focused on Irish dockworkers in *On the Waterfront*, which featured Marlon Brando as a tormented Irish boxer turned union goon.

One glaring exception to these rough-and-tumble urban Irish films was *Gone with the Wind* (1939). This classic is so often associated with Southern gentility that it is quite easy to forget that the heroine's name was, of course, Scarlett O'Hara. Her father even spoke with an obvious Irish accent in the film.

By the 1950s, though the Irish were advancing in America, films such as *The Young Philadelphians* (1959) were exploring conflicts that the Irish faced as they climbed the social ladder. Paul Newman played an ambitious young man raised by a mother who shamefully conceals his father's true identity: that of a working-class Irish politician. (*The Last Hurrah*, dating from 1958 and starring Spencer Tracy, showed how the old Irish political machines were actually fading.)

With Irish Americans assimilating and increasingly moving into the middle class, Hollywood turned to more historical Irish films. *The Molly Maguires* (1970), starring Sean Connery, told the story of the infamous 1870s labor union, and the immigration epic *Far and Away* (1992) explored how some Irish immigrants headed west.

New twists on old films also emerged at the end of the twentieth century. *Miller's Crossing* (1990), *GoodFellas* (1990), *State of Grace* (1990), and *The Road to Perdition* (2002) all put new spins on the old Irish gangster genre. Uniquely, *The Brothers McMullen* (1995)—which was written by, directed by, and starred Ed Burns—chronicled the religious, marital, and familial troubles of one contemporary Long Island family. Perhaps Burns's film will kick off a new phase of movies, in which suburbia is the setting for people and conflicts that remain uniquely Irish-American.

RIGHT: *Ed Burns makes movies about the trials and tribulations of Irish Americans in the suburbs.*

BELOW: *The gangster flick was revived in 1990's* GoodFellas. *Robert De Niro (left) and Ray Liotta (right) play Irish-Italian hoods who work with Italian mobster Joe Pesci.*

BELOW: *Tom Hanks played a tortured Chicago-area Irish gangster in* The Road to Perdition.

"THIS IS IRELAND, SEAN, NOT AMERICA"

In 1952, Hollywood took Irish Americans back to the old country with the most famous Irish-American movie ever made—director John Ford's *The Quiet Man*. What appears to be a simple, if occasionally raucous, love story has actually become quite controversial in Irish circles. Some feel that the depiction of Ireland in the movie is silly, sentimental, or even offensive (there is quite a bit of drinking and brawling).

Still, Ford's movie is revered by many as a classic. In *The Quiet Man*, retired boxer Sean Thornton (John Wayne) returns to his late mother's home in Ireland. There he falls in love with flame-haired, sharp-tongued Mary Kate Danaher (Maureen O'Hara).

John Ford (whose real name was Sean Aloysius O'Feeney) was one of America's great directors, creating other classics such as *Stagecoach* (1939), *The Grapes of Wrath* (1940), and *The Searchers* (1956). He worked regularly with the rugged John Wayne (whose real name was the not-so-rugged Marian Morrison) and also made several great Irish movies, including *The Informer* (1935) and *The Rising of the Moon* (1957).

The Quiet Man was an unusually tender Ford collaboration with Wayne (who was also Irish American). The sentimental view of Irish life also suggests that—as with romantic Irish music—Irish

ABOVE AND LEFT: *Director John Ford's* The Quiet Man *is perhaps the most famous Irish Hollywood film, though some people do not like its portrayal of Ireland. In the film, Wayne played an American-born boxer who has returned to his mother's Irish home, only to fall in love with Maureen O'Hara.*

Americans had set aside (or did not want to look at) impoverished, famine-scarred Ireland.

Those who love *The Quiet Man* for its fights and laughter, as well as those who hate the film for its stage Irish brogues, miss important details. The chemistry between Wayne and O'Hara is smoldering, as Sean struggles to understand this fierce woman and foreign country. "This is Ireland, Sean, not America," he is bluntly reminded at one point. Perhaps more importantly, the town's Catholics and Protestants come together in the end for a common cause. Ford, the son of an immigrant, liked to boast that he knew many Irish rebels. However, *The Quiet Man* actually echoes his hope for and vision of religious peace and harmony in Ireland.

BELOW AND RIGHT: *John Ford introduced John Wayne—and the classic American Western movie—to audiences with his 1939 epic* Stagecoach, *and later,* The Searchers *(1956).*

O'NEILL, FITZGERALD, AND IRISH-
AMERICAN LITERATURE

More than one critic has called Eugene O'Neill the American Shakespeare. And more than one critic has nominated *The Great Gatsby*, by F. Scott Fitzgerald, as the greatest American novel ever written. These authors, who both blossomed in the 1920s, were very different, but both men understood their work to be deeply Irish in nature.

O'Neill was the more obviously Irish. His father, James, was one of the greatest actors of his day, best known for his work as the Count of Monte Cristo. Though he was a wealthy man, James O'Neill, a famine immigrant, lived as though poverty always lurked around the corner. His son Eugene, meanwhile, was artistically inclined and far from being a typical working-class Irish-American of his day. By the time he wrote *Long Day's Journey into Night*, the long shadow of his Irish heritage was clear. In works such as *A Touch of the Poet* and *A Moon for the Misbegotten*, Eugene returned again and again to tragic Irish characters battling isolation, poverty, and alcoholism.

Fitzgerald, meanwhile, once said of himself, "I am half black Irish and half old American stock with the usual exaggerated ancestral pretensions." Also born into a financially secure family, Fitzgerald may not have written directly about Irish characters. However, many attribute the outsider struggles that are evident in both *The Great Gatsby*

and other works to Fitzgerald's Irish heritage, which was "straight 1850 potato-famine Irish," as the author himself put it. (Similarly, novelist John O'Hara's alienated characters of the 1930s to 1950s are reflections of the author's own Irish-Catholic youth in white Anglo-Saxon Protestant Pennsylvania.)

The greatest novelist of the Irish working class was James T. Farrell. His "Studs Lonigan" trilogy is a remarkably detailed look at Irish Chicago in the 1930s. Farrell's novels are far from complimentary, for many of his Irish characters are bitter, provincial, or suffocating under the strains of Catholicism. Still, his portrait of Irish-American life is unmatched. Meanwhile, Edwin O'Connor wrote the great Irish political novel *The Last Hurrah* and great priesthood novel *The Edge of Sadness*.

ABOVE: *Eugene O'Neill was haunted by family ghosts. His father left Ireland with his family during the famine.*

LEFT: *Jessica Lange and Charles Dance portrayed the doomed Tyrone parents in a memorable production of Eugene O'Neill's autobiographical play* A Long Day's Journey into Night.

LEFT: *James T. Farrell's "Studs Lonigan" trilogy is a harsh look at Chicago's working-class Irish in the 1930s.*

INK-STAINED AND IRISH

In June 1884, a Chicago 16-year-old named Finley Peter Dunne took a job as an errand boy at the *Chicago Telegram*. This was the first step in a career that would influence American journalism for well over a century.

Dunne, the son of Irish immigrants, would go on to become one of the most famous newspaper columnists of his era. He passed biting opinions through his character Martin J. Dooley, an Archer Avenue saloon keeper on Chicago's South Side. With his Irish brogue and his opinion on everything from politics to sports, Mr. Dooley dazzled readers throughout the 1890s. Finley Peter Dunne would be the first of many Irish-American

LEFT: *Pulitzer Prize-winner Jimmy Breslin led an impressive group of Irish-American journalists who began writing for top American newspapers in the 1950s and 1960s.*

journalists to write from the perspective of working-class Irish neighborhoods.

Given the Irish reverence for language (not to mention their knowledge of America's native tongue), the Irish were quick to start up ethnic newspapers in the early nineteenth century. By the 1870s, *Irish World* editor Patrick Ford was a leading voice for reform in Ireland and America. Meanwhile, Irish-American Nellie Bly (who was born Elizabeth Jane Cochran) was the first investigative journalist to disguise herself to get the inside scoop on a story.

Into the twentieth century, Irish journalists dominated big-city newsrooms from New York to San Francisco, telling colorful stories about neighborhood characters. The ethnic press maintained its powerful role, covering events in Ireland and Irish-American neighborhoods. The 1960s and 1970s became something of a golden age for Irish-American journalism, with the likes of Jimmy Breslin and Pete Hamill covering the New York scene. During the 1980s and 1990s, Irish-American columnists won four Pulitzer Prizes for commentary (Breslin at the *New York Daily News*, Jim Dwyer at *Newsday*, Eileen McNamara at the *Boston Globe*, and Anna Quindlen at the *New York Times*). To this day, though immigrants can get Ireland's finest daily newspapers on the Internet, many U.S. cities are still served by one, two, or even more Irish weekly newspapers.

THE MELTING POT

LEFT: *"Doing the Slums,"
a scene from the Five
Points, a New York
neighborhood where
Irish immigrants
interacted with different
ethnic groups.*

IMMIGRANT INTERACTION

In the smash-hit 1922 play *Abie's Irish Rose*, Abie and Rose Mary are a young New York couple who have just married. They live in a humble apartment, they do not make much money, and their neighborhood is a little rough. However, Abie and Rose Mary love each other very much, which is all that matters. That is not what their fathers think, however. Rose Mary's dad, Patrick Murphy, is outraged that his daughter would wed outside her clan, marrying a Jew. Abie's father,

Solomon, feels the same way, enraged that his son would marry an Irish-Catholic girl.

As *Abie's Irish Rose* suggests, by the 1920s Irish Americans were just one group in the famous American melting pot (the term itself is derived from the title of another early-twentieth-century play). So just how did Irish immigrants and their children get along with the Germans, Italians, Jews, and African Americans with whom they often shared city blocks?

Although many people looked down on the Irish, there were also some people on whom the

Irish themselves looked down, as the violent horror of the New York City Draft Riots suggests. More than 100 years later, Irish South Boston became infamous nationwide for its opposition to the busing in of African-American students to Irish neighborhoods. That is only part of the story, though, for many famine immigrants had cordial relationships with African Americans. In fact, one of the reasons why middle-class New Yorkers avoided the infamous Five Points slum was because romantic relationships between Irish immigrants and African Americans were not uncommon.

ABOVE: *Clashes between African Americans and Irish immigrants were often violent. This racist Harper's illustration depicts the tension between both groups.*

RIGHT: *One scholar suggests that tap dancing (performed here by Maurice and Gregory Hines) emerged as a combination of Irish and African-American dance traditions.*

One scholar has even suggested that tap dancing emerged from the Five Points as a mixture of Irish and African dance traditions.

On a smaller scale, Margaret Mary Healey Murphy, a wealthy Texan widow, founded a church, school, and hospital to serve San Antonio's African-American community. Additionally, Irish labor leaders who ran the Knights of Labor and other unions vigorously organized African-American workers (although other unions excluded African Americans). A final important fact was that northern cities, where the Irish dominated before World War II, did not have comparatively large African-American populations. African Americans mostly lived in the South (or segregated northern neighborhoods), which tended to limit interaction between African and Irish Americans.

Irish and German immigrants, on the other hand, saw far more interaction. Both groups came to the United States largely in the mid-nineteenth

century. Tensions arose that were rooted in religion. Many Germans, after all, followed the Lutheran faith, although problems occurred with German Catholics, as well. The American Catholic church was so thoroughly dominated by the Irish that, in 1886, German priests in Cincinnati, Milwaukee, and St. Louis petitioned the pope, seeking more control over Midwest Catholic affairs. Nevertheless, intermarriage between Irish and Germans ran high. Infamous senator Joseph McCarthy and New York archbishop Cardinal John O'Connor were among the many Americans of Irish-German descent.

Irish and Italian immigrants may have shared the same religious faith and lived in the same northeastern cities, but they often clashed over politics, jobs, or even organized crime turf. One enduring source of Italian–Irish tension was complaints that parishes had no Italian-speaking priests. One compromise had Irish parishioners celebrating mass before a church's main altar, while Italians worshipped in their native tongue in a lower chapel in the same church.

When the first large waves of Italian immigration came to the United States in the 1880s, many Irish had finally attained footholds in labor unions, police departments, or Democratic Party political machines. Often they were reluctant to yield their hard-earned clout to the newcomers. So, from Boston to Brooklyn, Italians often went it alone, establishing separate labor unions and political

LEFT: *Enjoying this New York St. Patrick's Day parade are (from left) Cardinal John O'Connor, actress Maureen O'Hara, former Police Commissioner Ben Ward, and former Mayor Ed Koch.*

ABOVE: *Cardinal John O'Connor was one of millions of Americans to claim Irish-German ancestry. Both groups came to the United States in large numbers during the mid-nineteenth century.*

clubs. Despite a large Italian-American population, Boston would not elect an Italian mayor until 1993, after a dozen Irishmen had ruled City Hall.

Irish–Italian tensions, of course, exploded into violence concerning gangsters. Deanie O'Banion and "Bugs" Moran suffered at the hands of Al Capone. New York's John Gotti made a name for himself in the 1970s by executing a low-level Irish hood named Jimmy McBratney. The fact remains that because both groups often lived in such close proximity and attended the same schools, the cities and their suburbs were quickly filled with Irish-Italian children, such as actor John Travolta and talk show host Regis Philbin.

Perhaps tensions ran highest in Irish-Jewish neighborhoods. During the Great Depression of the 1930s, radio priest Charles Coughlin became a hero to many Irish Americans. Millions tuned in to his radio program, to hear him rail in what many believed to be anti-Semitic tones. In New York, some Coughlinite members of a group calling itself the Christian Front attacked Jewish youths on street corners and even hatched a plot to bomb Jewish businesses in 1940. In November 1943, Newsweek made a cover story out of Irish Catholic–Jewish tensions in Boston, while poet Wallace Stegner wrote about them in the July 1944 edition of *Atlantic Monthly*.

RIGHT: *Millions tuned in to Father Charles Coughlin during his radio show. But many blamed the "radio priest" for exacerbating tensions between Irish and Jewish Americans.*

LEFT: *John Travolta (seen here in the 1994 film* Pulp Fiction) *is among the millions of Americans who share Irish and Italian heritage.*

Irish–Jewish tension was rooted in ancient theological conflicts as well as economic insecurity specific to 1930s and 1940s America. Many Irish felt that even though they had been in America longer, the Jews were doing better economically. A perception also existed that the Irish and the Jews held widely differing opinions on crucial political matters such as communism.

For all the tension, though, most Irish leaders (such as Boston's Frances Sweeney of the Irish American Defense Association) condemned anti-Semitism in any form. Religious divisions also subsided following World War II, when many Irish and Jewish Americans were united by the common goal of defeating Japan and the Nazis. Of course, quietly, many Jewish and Irish Americans did exactly what the young lovers did in *Abie's Irish Rose*—cast aside their old-world divisions in the name of American hope, prosperity, and, of course, children.

LEFT: *Gang warfare between Chicago's Irish and Italian mobsters turned bloody on February 14, 1929, when seven members of the Deanie O'Banion/"Bugs" Moran gang were executed during the St. Valentine's Day massacre.*

1945 TO THE PRESENT

GREAT YEARS FOR AMERICA

This was one Irish immigrant's recollection of a 1950s American wake—the traditional social gathering that is held just before an immigrant leaves Ireland for good. The bad economic times of the Great Depression and World War II slowed immigration to the U.S. from Ireland to a trickle. Many Irish instead made the shorter trip to England. However, by the 1950s, when the U.S. economy picked up while Ireland's remained stagnant, a whole new wave of Irish came to the United States.

> *"There were callers for two days and nights, when everybody was coming by, and parties and everything. It's sad, you know, it's sad. To think of breakin' up with your old chums. I then, well I just got to New York, when I got a telegram saying my father was dead. So I was very lonely, but there was nothing I could do— I was so far away. It's hard breaking away, but when you're young and you have to decide your future, you just can't turn back."*

From the end of World War II to 1961, nearly 20 percent of Ireland's population emigrated, with nearly 70,000 immigrants going to the United States. More than one-third of those went to New York City, where Irish enclaves could be found in the boroughs of Queens, Brooklyn, and the Bronx. Unlike many other immigrant groups, once the Irish came to America, they generally stayed for good. In the first decade of the twentieth century, just 2 percent of Irish immigrants returned home, in stark contrast to Italians, Swedes, Greeks, and others, who returned home in numbers as high as 60 percent.

FAR LEFT: *Irish immigrants who came to New York after World War II were greeted by Lady Liberty, and a much more crowded skyline than earlier immigrants had seen.*

LEFT: *Two boys talk things over in Queens, New York, a popular destination for 1950s Irish immigrants.*

So, as generations before had done, the 1950s Irish reinvigorated Irish neighborhoods. Ancient Order of Hibernians divisions, which might have closed, suddenly had new members. These also tended to be traditional, devout Catholics, not unlike the second- and third-generation Irish in America. Social halls that had not seen a *ceili* for years were suddenly holding monthly gatherings.

"The Irish who came over in the 1950s really tried to become Irish Americans," one author has written. "They joined the social clubs, forged neighborhoods . . . there was nothing to go back to Ireland to."

In September 1956, a new Manhattan dance hall, City Center, opened. Irish music was the club's top draw. Under the direction of Kerry native Bill

LEFT: *An Irish social group joins the procession during a 1955 ceremony to mark the end of an era. The Third Avenue "El" train was about to be torn down—one of many changes occurring in New York following World War II.*

RIGHT: *Irish immigration in the 1950s was very different from past eras in one major way—many immigrants could now fly to the United States.*

Fuller, 2,000 people a night often came to see musicians "direct from Ireland." However, the 1950s immigrant experience was different in certain ways. Some Irish now took planes to the United States (though it still could take 20 hours, with a refueling stop in Canada); others still sailed the Atlantic, though the days of the coffin ships were long gone.

Some things, though, remained the same. For many immigrants, the trip to America was the first time they had ever been off their rural farm.

Immigrants like Kevin Morrisey seemed to think it was all worth it. "Those were great years for America . . . a joyous period . . . the best period in the life of this country."

J. F. K.

Future senator Daniel Patrick Moynihan, and many other people, used the boxed quote following the assassination of John Fitzgerald Kennedy (J. F. K.) on November 22, 1963. It seemed to capture something poignant, tragic, and particularly Irish about the Kennedy clan as a whole. They were, of course, America's royal family. In a way, the election of J. F. K. as the nation's first Roman Catholic president marked the ultimate moment of triumph for the Irish in America.

Though the Irish Americans did not uniformly support Kennedy in 1960, the symbolism was impossible to ignore. After decades of digging ditches and cleaning homes and the awful anti-Catholic sentiment that marked the 1928 presidential defeat of Al Smith, an Irish Catholic now occupied the highest office in the land. It was enough to make the many

> *"What's the use of being Irish if the world doesn't break your heart?"*

BELOW: *John F. Kennedy, America's first Irish-Catholic president, shakes hands with Father Richard J. Casey prior to Kennedy's inauguration, January 1961.*

Irish-American lawyers, doctors, and teachers (and police officers, plumbers, and nurses) look around and say, "We've finally made it."

Of course, this triumph was achieved only following great tragedy. It began in Wexford in 1849 when Patrick Kennedy (J. F. K.'s great-grandfather) was forced to flee the famine, traveling for weeks on the same ship to Boston as his future wife, Bridget Murphy. Their son Patrick Joseph Kennedy Jr. scrimped and saved and became a successful saloon owner, marrying a "lace curtain" Irish girl named Mary August Hickey. Their firstborn, Joseph Patrick Kennedy, would marry Rose Elizabeth Fitzgerald, daughter of legendary Boston mayor John F. ("HoneyFitz") Fitzgerald. Rose and Joe raised nine children; five would meet tragic ends. Joe Jr. was killed during World War II, Kathleen was killed in a plane crash in 1948, and Rosemary suffered from mental retardation and was lobotomized.

So by the time war hero and Harvard graduate Jack was running for president, it finally seemed that the Fitzgeralds and the Kennedys could securely embrace American success. However, the question remained: could a Catholic win the White House, especially one with a father as controversial as Joe, often dismissed as an Irish bootlegger who had purchased his son's political power?

America, however, had grown more tolerant by 1960, although influential figures such as Norman Vincent Peale still warned against electing a Catholic president. "Our American culture is at stake . . . I don't say it won't survive, but it won't be what it was," Peale said, following a meeting of prominent and concerned Protestant leaders. Kennedy, however, bested Dwight Eisenhower's vice president Richard Nixon by 100,000 votes. (According to myth, mayor Richard Daley stole enough votes in Chicago to put Kennedy over the top. The truth is that even if J. F. K. had lost those

BELOW: *President Kennedy was greeted like a rock star during a trip to his ancestral home in Dunganstown, Ireland, in June 1963.*

Chicago votes, he would still have won the all-important state electoral vote with a landslide.)

President Kennedy was not just the young symbol of an optimistic nation. He was also the ultimate Irish politician, rising through the ranks of the Boston machine. "Be more Irish than Harvard," poet Robert Frost told the newly inaugurated president—and in many ways J. F. K. listened. He was hardly, it should be noted, a devout, observant Catholic. Not only did rumors fly about numerous extramarital affairs, but he also disagreed with church teaching on several key issues. Still, Kennedy's famous trip to his ancestral Irish home in June 1963 felt like a collective homecoming for millions of Irish Catholics.

So there was a sense of tragedy, almost like something out of Eugene O'Neill, when Kennedy was assassinated in Dallas. He was just 46 years old. Things got even worse when his brother Robert was also murdered in 1968. It was as if the Irish could attain success in America only if they paid a terrible price—whether that was one man's assassination or a famine that starved much of Ireland.

Some, of course, hoped that John F. Kennedy Jr. would carry his father's torch into old age. Unfortunately, he, too, ultimately met a tragic end. When his plane disappeared into the foggy skies over Massachusetts in 1999, John F. Kennedy Jr. was just 39 years old—even younger at his death than his father had been.

ABOVE: *Suburban life was different from life in close-knit city parishes—though in both places there were plenty of children.*

LEFT: *Thanks to the G.I. Bill and American prosperity in the 1950s, many Irish Americans bought homes in the suburbs.*

LEAVING THE PARISH

"My mother didn't want to leave the Bronx. Period," Brian McDonald recalls. When Brian's father, a New York police officer, proposed that the family move to the suburb of Pearl River, his wife Eleanor asked, only half jokingly, "Do they even have Catholics there?"

The 1950s and 1960s marked an era of great change for the Irish in America. They were leaving their old parishes and heading to the suburbs. This, of course, had been happening for more than a century. However, with one of their own in the White House, the last strongholds began to fall. Many Irish Americans had, by now, become their first family members to go to college. Children followed suit, whether or not it was to a Catholic college. Additionally, the young Irish did not seem quite as interested as their parents in *ceilis*, Catholicism, or parish life.

Some maintained strong ties to the old neighborhoods. However, by the 1960s, they would commute from the suburbs to work or to visit old friends. The Irish transition to the suburbs was not straightforward, however, with a home, lawn, and two-car garage at the end of some wonderful rainbow. Many Irish Americans, such as Eleanor McDonald, ached for the rituals of the old parish. Additionally, many heavily Protestant suburbs were not exactly thrilled at the influx of Irish-Catholic "city kids."

Irish Americans watched, with sadness or anger, as their old enclaves changed dramatically. The Irish were often replaced by poorer, more disadvantaged African or Hispanic Americans. Crime rose substantially. Many Irish police officers or firefighters (who resided in the suburbs) had to battle the ills of urban America (ills that, it should be noted, were not unlike those that had rankled Protestant America when the Irish dominated the slums).

Inevitably, such changes became political. Eleanor McDonald, for example, was an avid Irish J. F. K. Democrat, although her husband voted for Nixon. "As soon as a cop buys a power lawn mower he becomes a staunch republican," a saying went. "Jack Kennedy . . . was no Al Smith," writer Thomas Mallon noted. "Not only had he gone to Harvard, his father had gone to Harvard!"

By 1960, Irish Americans such as Dan Mahoney or Kieran O'Doherty favored neither political party. Mahoney went home one night and told his sharp-tongued wife Kathleen (née O'Doherty), "Kieran and I are

BELOW: *In 1962, Kieran O'Doherty (seen here voting) and other Irish Americans helped create the New York Conservative party, which dramatically signaled that the Irish were drifting away from the Democratic party.*

ABOVE AND RIGHT: *Policemen push along youths arrested at Chicago's Lincoln Park during the 1968 Democratic convention. Many Irish Americans—who had close ties to police officers all over the United States—were outraged at the era's antiwar demonstrators, rather than police accused of using excessive force.*

going to start a [third political] Party." Kathleen replied, "Have you got time for dinner first?" That two politically active Irishmen would eschew the Democrats and instead start up New York's Conservative Party might have seemed odd 50 years earlier. By 1960, it made sense: the Irish could afford to turn away from the Democratic Party.

Often this transition took place not inside some spacious suburban ranch but in modest, working-

LEFT: *Many Irish Americans proudly called themselves "Reagan Democrats." In 1980, Ronald Reagan was the first Republican to earn the support of many loyal Irish Democrats.*

class homes in residential Brooklyn or South Boston. From there, the increasing chaos of the 1960s—Vietnam, the subsequent antiwar protests, the urban riots, the counterculture on Ivy League campuses—seemed ominous to many Irish Americans. Respect for authority (a trademark in Irish America at least since the days of Dagger John Hughes) seemed to be vanishing. Many Irish in Chicago—and across America—cheered the heavy-handed way in which Richard Daley and the police treated the young protesters outside the 1968 Democratic convention, who, after all, were nothing like the Democrats who reared the Irish.

It might have seemed like a contradiction that some Irish Americans supported civil rights for oppressed Catholics in Northern Ireland but were more skeptical of the U.S. civil rights movement. By the late 1960s, though, civil rights in the United States had become tangled up with so many other complicated matters. Many Irish Americans found comfort in simply railing against the unjust Brits and defending the IRA. Meanwhile, they cheered U.S. Republican politicians such as California's governor (and former actor) Ronald Reagan, who made a name for himself baiting the radical students at Berkeley or San Francisco's hippie scene.

They may still have had a portrait of J. F. K. in their living room. However, when the president with the Irish name (even if he was not Catholic) swept into office in 1980, many Irish Americans proudly called themselves Reagan Democrats.

EPILOGUE

THE IRISH: OLD AND NEW

It is ironic that Irish Americans would help to send Frank McCourt's memoir, *Angela's Ashes*, soaring up the best-seller lists in 1997. At a time of great triumph for the Irish in America, they seemed to embrace a look back at their collective adversity. McCourt led the way for an Irish-American renaissance in the 1990s, marked by similarly popular Irish books, the dance extravaganza Riverdance, and the proliferation of everything from Irish parades and dance classes to Irish studies courses.

At the same time, a new wave of young Irish immigrants came to America in the 1980s and 1990s. They were younger, better educated, and certainly more hip than previous immigrants. (Things were not entirely different; Ireland's economy remained depressed in the 1980s and 1990s.) In the later 1990s, however, Ireland itself underwent a revolution. Its economy improved so quickly that Ireland became known as the Celtic Tiger. The "new Irish" generally eschewed dingy saloons, sometimes favoring Euro-flavored cafés, and never quite understood what was so grand about the green glasses and red-haired wigs of St. Patrick's Day. While some new immigrants did not see eye to eye with established Irish Americans, when the plight of illegal Irish immigrants gained attention in the late 1980s, Irish-American lawyers and politicians helped "legalize the Irish," as the chant went.

Meanwhile, in Irish political leader Gerry Adams, Irish Americans saw a figure who just might be able to help bring lasting peace to Northern Ireland after 30 years of renewed bloodshed in Ulster. The year 1997 marked the 150th anniversary of the worst year of the Irish Famine. Many felt that the Irish had, once and for all, finally put the hunger behind them. Did that mean that Irish culture in America might die? Actor/author Malachy McCourt (Frank's brother) offered as good an answer as any. At a solemn reception marking the opening of the stirring Irish Famine memorial in downtown Manhattan, McCourt quipped, "Death, to the Irish, is not always fatal."

FRANK MCCOURT,
Angela's Ashes

"Worse than the miserable ordinary childhood is the miserable Irish childhood, and worse still is the miserable Irish-Catholic childhood."

LEFT: *Sinn Fein leader Gerry Adams (center) helped usher in a tenuous, but precious, era of peace in Northern Ireland, after decades of bloodshed.*

FAR LEFT: *At a time of Irish-American prosperity, Frank McCourt's lyrical memoir of misery and woe struck a chord with readers.*

BELOW: *Irish dancing—popularized by the smash show Riverdance—became a cultural phenomenon during the 1990s.*

TIMELINE

1580s Irishman John Nugent joins Sir Walter Raleigh on the explorer's expedition to the future North Carolina region.

1649 Oliver Cromwell leads a notorious British military expedition to crush a rebellion by Catholics in Ireland.

1760s Earliest St. Patrick's Day parade held in New York.

1770 Dublin native Patrick Carr is one of five men killed in the Boston Massacre.

1776 Anti-Catholic laws are passed throughout the American colonies. The

BELOW: *Irish-Americans played a large part in the first fighting force, the militia.*

Declaration of Independence is printed by County Tyrone immigrant John Dunlap. Three signatories (all Protestant) are Irish-born.

1798 Wolfe Tone leads Irish rebels in an attempt to overthrow British rule in Ireland. Two years later, the Act of Union tightens Britain's colonial grip on Ireland.

1825 The Erie Canal opens. Irish immigrants are prominent among the canals' laborers.

1828 Andrew Jackson, the son of Scotch-Irish immigrants, is elected U.S. President.

1829 The Catholic Emancipation Act is passed in Ireland. However, poor economic times and land disputes force more Irish Catholics to emigrate.

1834 An angry mob burns a Catholic convent in Massachusetts. This is just one of many bouts of anti-Irish Catholic violence to break out in northeastern U.S. cities.

1836 The first Division of the Ancient Order of Hibernians is founded in the United States.

1847 The first year of a horrific famine in Ireland. Over the next few years, more than 1 million Irish will emigrate, and another 1.5 million will die.

1849 A "Gold Rush" in the American west sends many poor Irish immigrants to California and the west coast.

1850s One of the most popular political movements is the anti-Catholic, anti-immigrant group the "Know Nothings."

RIGHT: *Grace Kelly, successful actress-turned-princess, was descended from Irish-German immigrants.*

1861–65 The U.S. Civil War; 150,000 Irish immigrants fight for the Northern Union, while 30,000 fight for the Southern Confederacy.

1863 The New York City Draft Riots; many rioters are Irish laborers, angry that they (but not wealthy Americans) will be drafted into a Civil War they do not support.

1867 Frank McCoppin is the first Irish-Catholic immigrant elected mayor of a major U.S. city, San Francisco.

1880s New York and Boston elect Irish-Catholic mayors, thanks to Irish-dominated political organizations. City police and fire departments also become largely Irish.

1916 The Easter Rebellion in Ireland spurs a new revolutionary movement and war. By 1921, the British no longer rule the 26 counties of southern Ireland.

1928 Al Smith becomes the first Irish Catholic to run for president. He is opposed by the anti-Catholic Ku Klux Klan.

1941–45 World War II; Irish Americans fight alongside other immigrants and ethnic groups on the front lines.

1952 A sluggish economy in Ireland and a flourishing U.S. economy spur a new wave of immigration from Ireland.

1960 John F. Kennedy becomes America's first Irish-Catholic president.

Late 1960s A new civil rights movement for Catholics in Northern Ireland leads to British resistance, bloodshed, and violence.

1972 A civil rights march in Northern Ireland turns deadly when 13 Catholic marchers are shot by British soldiers. "Bloody Sunday," starts a new wave of Catholic–Protestant violence in the north, where the IRA wages a terrorist campaign against British rule.

1997 Irish Americans commemorate the 150th anniversary of the Irish Famine with solemn memorials. A new peace process is afoot in Ireland, with the IRA and other groups declaring a ceasefire.

1998 The Good Friday peace accord ushers in an era of tenuous, but hopeful, peace in Northern Ireland.

RESOURCES

BOOKS

Almeida, Linda Dowling, *Irish Immigrants in New York City, 1945–1995*, Indiana University Press, 2001.

Anbinder, Tyler, *The Nineteenth Century New York City Neighborhood That Invented Tap Dance, Stole Elections, and Became the World's Most Notorious Slum*, Free Press, New York, 2001.

Bayor, Ronald H., and Meagher, Timothy J. (eds), *The New York Irish*, Johns Hopkins University Press, Baltimore, 1996.

Freedman, Samuel G., *The Inheritance: How Three Families and America Moved from Roosevelt to Reagan and Beyond*, Simon and Schuster, New York, 1996.

Gamm, Gerald, *Urban Exodus: Why the Jews Left Boston and the Catholics Stayed*, Harvard University Press, Cambridge, 1999.

Glazier, Michael (ed.), *The Encyclopedia of the Irish in America*, Notre Dame University Press, Notre Dame, 1999.

Golway, Terry, *For the Cause of Liberty: A Thousand Years of Ireland's Heroes*, Touchstone, New York, 2001.

———, *So Others Might Live: A History of New York's Bravest, The FDNY from 1700 to the Present*, Basic Books, New York, 2002.

Golway, Terry, and Coffey, Michael (eds.), *The Irish in America*, Hyperion, New York, 1997.

Lardner, James, and Repetto, Thomas, *The NYPD: A City and its Police*, Henry Holt & Company, New York, 2001.

Llywelyn, Morgan, *A Pocket History of Irish Rebels*, O'Brien Press Ltd., Dublin, 2000.

Mangan, James J. (ed.), *Robert Whyte's 1847 Famine Ship Diary. Journey of an Irish Coffin Ship*, Irish American Book Company, Maryland, 1997.

McDonald, Brian, *My Father's Gun: One Family, Three Badges, One Hundred Years in the NYPD*, Plume, New York, 2000.

Miller, Kerby, and Miller, Patricia Mulholland, *Journey of Hope: The Story of Irish Immigration to America*, Chronicle, San Francisco, 2001.

O'Donnell, Edward T., *1001 Things Everyone Should Know About Irish American History*, Broadway, New York, 2002.

Ó hEithir, Breandán, *A Pocket History of Ireland*, O'Brien Press Ltd., Dublin, 2000.

Padden, Michael, and Sullivan, Robert (eds.), *May the Road Rise to Meet You: Everything You Need to Know about Irish American History*, Plume, New York, 1999.

Slayton, Robert A., *Empire Statesman: The Rise and Redemption of Al Smith*, Free Press, New York, 2001.

WEB SITES

Ancient Order of Hibernians (www.aoh.com) provides information on the Catholic group in America.

Embassy of Ireland (www.irelandemb.org) offers thorough links on Irish and Irish-American media, tourism, government offices, and more.

Irish Abroad (www.irishabroad.com) offers information on genealogy and Irish people and events all over the world.

Irish America Net (www.irishamericanet.com) offers information about Irish-American events across the United States.

Irish Music Studies (www.ul.ie/~iwmc/programmes/ims/index.html) is from the University of Limerick.

Irish Search (www.irishsearch.net) is a search engine for Irish and Irish-American news, cultural groups, and tourism.

"Long Journey Home" (www.pbs.org/wgbh/pages/irish) is the web site for the PBS Irish in America documentary, with information of people, music, and more.

When in doubt, check these sites, with thousands of links all across the United States:

Open Directory Project (dmoz.org/Society/Ethnicity/Irish)

Yahoo! Directory of Irish-American Culture (dir.yahoo.com/Regional/Countries/United_States/Society_and_Culture/Cultures_and_Groups/Cultures/American__United_States_/Irish_American)

Yahoo! Directory of Irish Cultural Groups (dir.yahoo.com/Society_and_Culture/Cultures_and_Groups/Cultures/Irish)

MUSEUMS AND CULTURAL GROUPS

Glucksman Ireland House, New York University
1 Washington Mews
New York NY 10003
Tel: 212-998-3950
www.nyu.edu/pages/irelandhouse

Irish American Center
4626 N. Knox Avenue
Chicago, IL 60630
Tel: 773-282-7035
www.irishamhc.com

Irish American Cultural Institute
1 Lackawanna Place
Morristown, New Jersey NJ 07960
Tel: 973-605-1991
www.irishaci.org

Irish American Historical Society, 991 Fifth Avenue
New York City, NY 10028
Tel: 212-288-2263
Also has a California branch: Tel: 805 565 3259
www.aihs.org

Irish Cultural Center
200 New Boston Drive
Canton, MA 02021
Tel: 781-821-8291 or 1-888-GO-IRISH
www.irishculture.org

INDEX

Author's Acknowledgments

This book is dedicated to the memory of my father, Tom Sr., and future of my daughter, Maggie. I would like to thank the great New York writer Terry Golway for years of help, as well as "the handoff." Thanks to Niall O'Dowd and Georgina Brennan at the *Irish Voice* and Trish Harty at *Irish America* magazine. Special thanks to my wife Kate, who does all the real work. Finally, thanks to family named Deignan, Murphy, Hughes and Jordan (not to mention DeSantis, Gonzalez, and Huangs) for showing me how the Irish lived in America.